SPECIAL OFFA

WALKING THE OFFA'S DYKE PATH

Bob Bibby

Published by Eye Books

Special Offa
First Edition
June 2004

Published by Eye Books Ltd
51a Boscombe Rd
London
W12 9HT
Tel/fax: +44 (0) 20 8743 3276
website: www.eye-books.com

Set in Frutiger and Garamond
ISBN: 1903070287

British Library Cataloguing in Publication Data
A catalogue record for this book is available from the British Library

Printed and bound in Great Britain by Biddles Ltd

To Enid again

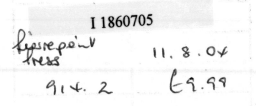

Acknowledgements

Special thanks to the following: Martin Clare, Tom Dewhurst and Roger Lamming for their company; Rev. Beth Torkington of Brockweir Moravian Church, Rev. Jean Prosser of St Cadoc's Church in Llangattock Lingoed, Don Burgess of Freeminer Brewery and Justin 'Buster' Grant of Breconshire Brewery for additional information; Ceinwen Richards of Drewin Farm, Linda and Sarah Whitticase of Llwyn House in Montgomery, Ced and Jill Deathridge of the Golden Cross in Four Crosses, Roger Honey of Cambrian House in Llangollen, Gwladys and Derek Edwards of Fron Haul in Sodom for kindness beyond the call of duty; all the other nameless or half-named people I met on my journey who added to my happiness in ways they may not have appreciated; and finally my wife, without whom none of it would have been possible.

Contents

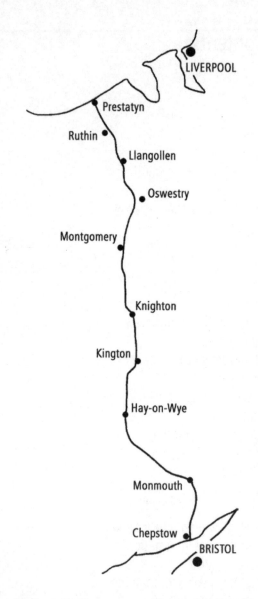

MAP OF THE OFFA'S DYKE PATH

1 Offa

"Bugger Offa," said my wife.

"That's it!" I exclaimed, leaping on to the coffee table and executing a neat, if I may say so, Irish jig thereon.

"That's what?" my wife asked.

"The title for the book," I explained mid-jig. "It's perfect. Just what I've been looking for. Slick. Racy. Post-modern. Catches the eye. Bugger Offa. It's perfect."

"The Women's Institutes won't like it," my wife pointed out witheringly. "So you can forget about them inviting you to speak to them. And I don't expect your publisher chappie will be happy with it either. Anyway that wasn't what I meant."

My spirits, so recently heightened, were already beginning to droop as I climbed from the table.

"What did you mean?" I asked.

"I meant I'm fed up with you rabbiting on about Offa," she explained. "All I've heard for the past year is Offa, Offa, Offa. I'm fed up with him. What's so special about him anyway?"

"Rex Anglorum," I began. "The very first person to proclaim himself so. King of the Angles. "

"Sounds more like a snooker player to me."

"But don't you realise," I continued, well into my stride now and ignoring her feeble attempt at humour, "all those England football fans, with their shaven heads and large wobbly bellies, chanting 'ANGLE-LAND, ANGLE-LAND, ANGLE-LAND', owe their origins to Offa."

"You mean those clowns who get drunk on German lager and drape themselves in the flag of the Turkish St George?" my wife asked. "Anyway, I bet half of them aren't even English. I hate all this phoney patriotism that comes with football. We're a nation of immigrants anyway, aren't we?"

"Well, I used to think so too till I came across this research from University College in London. They compared a sample of men from England with those from an area of the Netherlands where the Anglo-Saxons are thought to have originated and found the English had genes that were almost identical. It seems that even nowadays a large part of the genetic profile of the English is Anglo-Saxon. But, and this is a big but, they found that the Welsh males studied had a different genetic profile, suggesting that the Anglo-Saxon invaders were responsible for a sort of ethnic cleansing of Britain and that they drove the original inhabitants into Wales."

"So that's why Offa built his dyke?"

"Exactly," I concluded. "It's quite likely that the dyke acted as a genetic barrier as well as a physical one. That's why Offa matters. That's why I'm fascinated by him."

"So when are you going to walk the Dyke?" she asked. "It's a bit tougher than the walks you've done before, isn't it?

"I've cleared my diary for the end of June. And yes, it is tougher. And that's why I have to get into training for this one," I replied. "From Easter I need to be out every day, building up my strength and stamina."

"And then going to the pub every lunchtime to ruin it all."

My wife knows me well.

"No. Strict training. Not a drop will touch my lips from now till then," I boasted.

"It doesn't have time to touch your lips the way you drink."

I ignored this cutting remark

"But if I'm going to walk the Dyke, then I have to know more about Offa. That's why I'm reading all this stuff."

"Okay," she said. "But if you're going to write about it, please don't call your book Bugger Offa."

I sighed. It had seemed such a good idea.

The type of schooling I had, which I guess was, and probably still is, pretty common in England, gave me a view of history which was not far removed from the comic version in Sellars's and Yeatman's *1066 and All That*. In other words, the early history of Britain was defined by two moments, viz. the landing of Julius Caesar (*veni, vidi, vici* - or I came, I bought the video, I did a spot of vice) and the defeat of Harold (*On his 'orse with his 'awk in his 'and*) at the Battle of Hastings in 1066. The first event saw the coming of the Romans and led to the dominance of Rome for four hundred years, while the second event saw the arrival of William and the Norman Conquerors who stayed quite a lot longer.

What this version of history didn't do, of course, was give me any idea of what happened in between the departure of the Roman legions to return to Italy, in order to invent spaghetti bolognese, pointy-toed shoes and the Fiat Cinquecento, and the arrival of the Norman French with their *haute cuisine*, garlic breath and black berets. This period is usually, and quite unjustly, referred to as the Dark Ages, not because the peoples who arrived on these shores during that period were dark-skinned but because they were illiterate. Consequently, we have few written records from this time. What we do have are the writings of various churchmen, such as the Venereal Bede, and later compilations, such as the *Anglo-Saxon Chronicle* (a forerunner of the *News of the World*). The records are incomplete and the versions of history are quite often contradictory but it is from these writings and their subsequent interpretations by experts that we are able to piece together something about the period up to and including Offa, the first King of the Angles.

Now there are far clearer and fuller descriptions of this period of history than I intend to give you here. All I'm going to say is that there appears to have been a pretty huge migration of peoples from Scandinavia and Germany into Britain between the retirement of the Romans and Offa's accession to the throne of Mercia in AD 757. The Mercians, who were the top dogs now, had originally been part of the Angle invasion to the east of the country and their original sphere of influence appears to have been in the Trent valley but over the years they spread further and further westwards and became more and more dominant in what we would now call middle England. The Mercians brought with them their gods, naturally, amongst whom were Tiw, Woden, Thor and Frigg and they give us Tuesday, Wednesday, Thursday and Friday.

The first great Mercian ruler was Penda (not to be confused with Pendant, Pennant or Earring) who defeated the West Saxons, managed by Thomas Hardy, and the Northumbrians, managed by Sir Bobby Robson, in the early seventh century. Almost a hundred years later Ethelbald, despite having a name like a follicly-challenged girlie, had a similarly high profile and was effectively in control of most of England south of the River Humber, though he was not much liked by the Christian missionary Archbishop Boniface who wrote to Ethelbald thus:

"...you have, as many say, neither taken a lawful wife nor maintained chaste abstinence for God's sake, but, governed by lust, have stained the fame of your glory before God and men by the sin of lasciviousness and adultery...And yet, what is worse, those who tell us this add that this shameful crime is especially committed in monasteries with holy nuns and virgins consecrated to God."

Bit of a randy old goat, eh?

But it is his successor, Offa, ruler from 757 to 796, who is the real subject of my narrative. What was Offa really like? We can only guess. The figure of him behind glass at the Offa's Dyke Centre in Knighton suggests he was a bit glum. A tapestry of the period, showing him mounted and in battledress surrounded by what looks like the Anglo-Saxon version of Kenny Ball's Jazz Band, paints a picture of a rather ferocious character with skinny legs. From the historical evidence it is clear that he was certainly vigorous and successful in establishing unity of control over the different tribes of Angle-land, and Welsh schoolchildren are still brought up to believe he was a nasty bastard. However, although we don't have much by way of public record of him, it is possible to document a number of indisputable facts about him.

First of all, he was the first to be referred to as *rex anglorum*, King of the English. Quite when this began is not known but it may have been shortly after he fought the Kentish armies at Otford in 776, a battle recorded thus in the *Anglo-Saxon Chronicle*:

"In this year a red cross appeared in the sky after sunset. And that year the Mercians and the people of Kent fought at Otford. And marvellous adders were seen in Sussex."

The last is believed to refer to a visitation from a team of accountants from the Mercian version of the Audit Commission.

Secondly, Offa had a profound impact on the development of trade with Europe and beyond and England became an internationally recognised power. The evidence for this claim is largely from correspondence between Charlemagne, the Holy Roman Emperor, and Offa (written in Latin by scribes, of course), in which the former offers protection for English sales reps. travelling round Europe in their Vauxhall Vectras. Charlemagne also complains about the length of the coats being sent abroad from England, though presumably Offa was merely anticipating Carnaby Street in trying to create a fashion for the mini-coat ahead of his time. Offa was also responsible for enhancing the coinage of his kingdom, making it so that it was acceptable for trading in Europe. These new coins were going to be called euros but at the last minute he changed this to pennies and they have persisted, in name at least, until our day. An example has also been found of a coin modelled on the Arabian dinar with Offa's name stamped on it, showing that English sales reps. were trading very far afield.

Thirdly, Offa had established strong relationships with the Pope, to such an extent that, when he had a barney with his Archbishop of Canterbury, Jaenberht, a Kentish man, he persuaded the Pope to allow the creation of a second Archbishopric at Lichfield in 787. This permitted Offa to take the highly unusual step of having his son Ecgfrith anointed to succeed to the throne. Mind you, this didn't help much as Ecgfrith only survived his father by six months.

Fourthly, and centrally for my story, Offa built his dyke. The monk Asser, writing his *Life of Alfred* in 893 almost a hundred years after Offa's death, reports thus:

"There was in Mercia in fairly recent times a certain vigorous king called Offa, who terrified all the neighbouring kings and provinces around him, and who had a great dyke built between Wales and Mercia from sea to sea."

And that is the oldest record we have of the existence of Offa's Dyke - there are no contemporary accounts of how or why it was built. Offa himself couldn't write, of course, and neither could any of his henchmen. After all, that's why they lived in the Dark Ages. Later writers refer to a legend that any Welshman found beyond the Dyke would have his hand or foot cut off and, as modern DNA research has shown, it certainly seems to have acted as a genetic barrier between the Welsh and the English. But for a better understanding of Offa's Dyke we have to rely on the interpretations of latter-day experts.

Okay, let's begin with a description. Offa's Dyke is nearly 150 miles long - just remember that's longer than the two Roman walls in northern Britain put together - and nearly 80 miles of it still exist, remarkably since it has never been of apparent interest to historians until relatively modern times. It begins south of Chepstow on Sedbury Cliffs overlooking the breadth of the River Severn as it becomes the Bristol Channel and travels pretty much due north to just south of Monmouth. There is then apparently a gap of some 37 miles where the experts think the River Wye may have acted as the barrier between the Welsh and the English. From this point, near Kington, the Dyke is almost continuous until near Welshpool, where there is another gap, possibly filled by the River Severn. The Dyke appears again for several stretches north of Welshpool, bypassing Oswestry and Wrexham before apparently petering out some10 miles short of the sea.

Excavations have shown that the Dyke was originally a six-foot deep ditch with a bank towering above it on the English side of 25 feet. The bank was constructed from the soil dug from the ditch together with stones and turves used to reinforce it. The ditch was V-shaped with a 45° angle up the face of the ditch and the bank, making it very difficult to climb over and almost impossible to drive livestock over.

The Offa's Dyke Centre in Knighton gives the following explanation of how the Dyke was built:

1. A rough line was set using bonfires or beacons.
2. This line was more accurately marked using stakes.
3. A plough was then run along to mark this line.
4. One man from every manor in Mercia was requisitioned.
5. Each man brought his own tools - primitive picks and shovels - bringing provisions from his manor to support him.
6. The earth from the ditch was piled up to form the bank.
7. Each man was responsible for building 125 cm, and then could go home.

Now this also is speculative, of course, but its simplicity appeals to me so I'm going with it. I'm quite fond of this picture of young Ceolred with his bucket and spade setting off from Hereford or Repton, his bag of fish-paste sandwiches and a jug of mead over his shoulder, ready for a spot of Dyke-digging in the borderlands. Maybe he'd get a chance to shout Anglo-Saxon obscenities at some Welsh farmers or, even better, find himself a Welsh shepherdess for a bit of cymru nookey.

Whatever. So much is just guesswork. We don't even know exactly when the Dyke was built, although it seems likely it was between 784 and Offa's death in 796. Almost certainly it would have taken several years because the scope of the enterprise was huge - there is not another structure of its kind anywhere else. And there have been equal amounts of speculation about the purpose of the Dyke, though I think most people agree now that it was a defensive barrier, designed to keep the Welsh boyos out of England.

It's remarkable really that such a huge structure should pass into the geographical and historical story of Britain with little or no documentation or comment. Indeed, until Sir Cyril Fox published the results of his 1920s and 1930s excavations on the

Dyke in 1955, there was very little public interest, understanding or knowledge of it or its whereabouts. Gerald of Wales, writing in 1194, includes the Dyke as one of the atrocities the English kings have committed against the Welsh, but being a Taff he would say that, wouldn't he? John Leland, the "king's antiquary" appointed by Henry VIII to search for all church records, notes it as being visible a few miles from Shrewsbury. There are other mentions in various specialised topographies in the ensuing centuries, many of which confuse other smaller dykes with Offa's earthwork. But overall there is a stunning silence about the Dyke.

That all changed in 1969 with the formation of the Offa's Dyke Association to campaign for the opening up of a long-distance footpath along the line of the Dyke, which led in 1971 to the official opening of the Offa's Dyke Path, a waymarked trail of 177 miles from Chepstow to Prestatyn. For over 60 miles of its length the path follows the actual Dyke, which in places is still almost 20 feet high from its ditch to the top of its bank. Since 1971, the Offa's Dyke Path has been walked by thousands and in the summer of 2003 I set out on my journey through time to witness at first hand this wonderful creation of the eighth century and its very special king - Offa.

Note for previous readers, wannabe anoraks and other old farts:

Readers of my first travel book, *Grey Paes and Bacon*, will recall that I set out on that journey around the canals of the Black Country in some trepidation because of a gammy left knee and readers of my second book, *Dancing with Sabrina*, will recall that I finished that walk down the length of the River Severn with a damaged right ankle. The latter turned out to be a torn Achilles tendon and, as with the knee previously, required some remedial treatment from my physiotherapist, the lovely Sharon. So, determined not to cause further damage to myself this time round, I actually got into training. For six weeks before I set off, I was out pounding the mean streets near my home in Bridgnorth, gradually increasing the distance and speed of my walking, till I could comfortably cover eight miles in a couple of hours.

Now this sort of thing is remarkably boring to do but it did serve to strengthen my feet and legs and remind my heart and lungs of what they were capable. I'm pleased to say that throughout the length of my walk along Offa's Dyke, I acquired no blisters nor any other damage, despite walking pretty much non-stop for two weeks and on some days covering almost 20 miles.

One major addition to my equipment for this jaunt was a walking pole, kindly purchased by my wife at great expense. I have to admit that, prior to receiving it, I had been typically old-fart-sniffy about such things. I'd watched people come bounding over hillsides or past my home overlooking the River Severn with these things and thought '*Poseurs*'. But, in reality, I found that it was really good to have another point of contact with the ground on hillsides; going up, it provides leverage, while going down, it provides stability. It was also, I discovered on my journey, a source of great comfort when meeting livestock along the route. One wave of my pole, accompanied by a trenchant shout of "Bugger Offa!" was enough to clear even the most recalcitrant herd of bullocks out of my way. A final unexpected use was as a fly swat, waved in front of my sweat-encrusted face, as I marched through hot and humid country lanes.

As far as other preparations, I naturally checked out the CAMRA *Good Beer Guide* first of all in order to ensure that, wherever possible, I could call in at some pubs serving decent beer on most of the days of my journey. Then, using the excellent *Where to Stay* booklet from the Offa's Dyke Association, I booked my bed and breakfast accommodation in advance, for on some parts of the path this is scanty. Finally, kitted out appropriately and armed with the official *Offa's Dyke Path National Trail Guides* and the relevant Ordnance Survey maps, I was ready.

As to why I did it, well, of course, Offa was just the excuse. Though a specially good one, I have to say, as I hope you'll see as you read on. But some of the rationale was to do with the feeling that those previous injuries might be turning me prematurely into an old fart. I wanted to show myself, and those who care for me, that I can still hack it. And I did it!

And now you'll want to know all about it, won't you?

2 Chepstow

I arrived in Chepstow, where the Offa's Dyke Path begins, late on a hot Sunday afternoon the day after Midsummer's Day and went to explore the town. It's an attractive little town, once you venture into its interior, with its old Town Gate, remnants of its Port Wall, the old streets around Beaufort Square and of course its Norman Castle. But it was to its museum that I headed first.

Now, if your first sight of a black sheriff was Black Bart, played by cool dude Cleavon Little, in Mel Brooks's hilarious cowboy spoof *Blazing Saddles*, than you will be very surprised to discover that he had an illustrious forebear. And this black sheriff lived in Chepstow, South Wales, not in the Wild West of the USA. His name was Nathaniel Wells and his story was told in a temporary exhibition in the fascinating Chepstow Museum.

Nathaniel Wells's father was one William Wells, who in 1749 had emigrated from Cardiff to St Kitts in the West Indies when he was 19 years old and there proceeded to make himself a very rich man through his ownership of extensive sugar plantations. In the process of building his fortune, he married a woman much older than himself and after her early death did what lots of respectable white slave owners did - he started shagging and impregnating his female slaves. He fathered two children by a slave named Perron, one by another named Sue, one by another named Sarah, and three by a woman known as Juggy. Nathaniel was the third of Juggy's offspring, born in 1779, and for some reason he became William Wells's favourite, being made a free man, adopted as his son and then sent to London to be educated.

William Wells died of dropsy in 1794. In his will he left money to several of his black women slaves, including Juggy who now had enough to have her own slaves. However, the bulk of his vast estate was left to "my natural and dear son Nathaniel Wells whose mother is my woman Juggy" when he reached the age of 21. Shortly after he finally inherited, Nathaniel Wells bought Piercefield House just outside Chepstow and installed his new wife Harriet there, becoming a pillar of the local community. He was a churchwarden at St Arvans church, an active member of the Chepstow Hunt, and a Justice of the Peace, while his plantations continued to bring him untold wealth and while Harriet produced eight children. When she died, Nathaniel promptly remarried and his new wife Esther gave him another 11 children over the next 15 years.

His appointment as the first black sheriff came in 1810 but was not remarked upon, despite the fact that a contemporary diarist described Nathaniel as "so much a man of colour as to be little removed from a Negro". Racist attitudes always disappear when the person you thought was different behaves exactly the way you do. Nathaniel was an English gentleman, a man of property and a man with prodigious breeding powers. He was to be envied rather than rejected. What is perhaps more curious is that he, the black son born into slavery, was an anti-abolitionist himself in the period immediately preceding William Wilberforce's Act which outlawed slavery.

Blazing Saddles opens with Black Bart, in response to the request for a negro spiritual, leading his fellow chain gangers in a silky-smooth rendition of Cole Porter's *I Get a Kick Out of You*. I don't know what sheriff Nathaniel Wells might have sung, but it would probably have been something from *Hymns Ancient and Modern*. So if you want to check out Black Bart's illustrious predecessor, go and have a look in Chepstow Museum.

Another remarkable story is told in the museum - that of Able Seaman William Charles Williams who was awarded the Victoria Cross posthumously in 1915 for his bravery at the landing on Gallipoli. Now you often hear mention of Gallipoli in reference to the First World War but it is not often pointed out that this was another glorious cock-up by the British High Command. The reason for the attempted landings at Gallipoli was because the British wanted to re-establish supply lines to their Russian allies via the Dardanelles (they didn't know that Lenin was waiting in the wings to take over, of course). So in April 1915 troops were sent in ships to take control of several beaches at Gallipoli.

Able Seaman Williams was on board the former Glasgow coal-boat HMS River Clyde whose task was to disembark troops using several barges as bridges for the soldiers to go from the ship to the shore. Unfortunately, the barges failed to reach their intended positions, with the result that a gap developed between them, making it impossible for the men to cross. Williams together with Commander Unwin waded waist deep in the water and in constant fierce gunfire sought to tow the barges together by rope which was not long enough and, while waiting for more rope, Williams was shot and killed. He had been in the water holding the rope for up to one hour.

The story is told in a glass display cabinet which also contains photographs of a fresh-looking Williams and of his proud parents receiving the Victoria Cross from King George V. There's a rather fine version of the incident in the cabinet in a book entitled *Deeds That Thrill the Empire*, complete with stirring drawings in the style of the time. There's also a copy of a painting of the attempted landing of HMS River Clyde - the original being in the town's parish church.

The story that isn't told, however, is of the disaster that was Gallipoli. The April landings were only partially successful and the Turkish troops remained in command of the Dardanelles. The quick advance that had been planned failed to happen and a replica of the northern France trench warfare began to develop. More British troops, but not enough, were sent to Suvla Bay to begin a further assault but they too failed to capture the ground that was so dearly desired. By the end of the year the British commanders had to admit defeat and by January 1916 the troops had been evacuated and another disgraceful chapter in British military history had been written. 46,000 allied soldiers had been killed during the fighting on land from a total of 250,000 casualties. The Turkish forces suffered losses that were possibly even greater.

The sadness and stupidity of war never fails to amaze me, even though it throws up hapless heroes like Able Seaman Williams VC.

It was different warfare that was responsible for the most prominent and dominant building in Chepstow - its castle. It was originally constructed on the orders of William fitz "Ozzie" Osbern, who was a close mate of William the Conqueror. Indeed, some would argue that it was Ozzie who recommended that William should fire his arrow into Harold's eye at Hastings and thus bring about the Norman Conquest. Not for Ozzie the foolhardiness of the minstrel and nut case Taileffer, the archetypal suicide bomber who advanced in front of the Norman formation to encourage them, shouting "Liberté, egalité, fraternité" and became the first casualty of the battle because he was hundreds of years ahead of his time. Not for Ozzie the remoteness of Bishop Odo, William's half-brother, who spent the whole of 1066 embroidering his version of the battle on the Bayeux Tapestry. No, Ozzie was right at the heart of William's War Cabinet - he's the one with the beard in the Bayeux Tapestry - and for his reward after the conquest was given the rich and fertile border lands of the Welsh Marches.

Ozzie built a formidable army with Hereford as his main base. He established castles and garrisons at Monmouth, Clifford and Wigmore, but his greatest work was the magnificent castle at Chepstow on the mouth of the river Wye. Chepstow was important because it gave control of the seaward approaches into Wales, its position spanning the River Wye and the River Severn meant it was crucial for controlling trade, and it provided a springboard into Wales. What is unusual about Chepstow Castle is that it is believed that this was the first stone castle built by the Normans. Most of the early castles they erected in the aftermath of 1066 were of the standard school history-book motte and bailey type, but for some reason, probably because the Welsh were seen to be more troublesome than the rest of the kingdom's inhabitants, Ozzie ordered a stone construction. The castle's Great Hall was begun in 1067 and still stands today, the oldest surviving stone castle of its type in Britain.

Of course, what you see now - the still magnificent shell of the castle buildings that dominate the skyline above the River Wye - is the result of many significant alterations, additions and amendments by subsequent residents of the castle and you really need to get hold of the excellent guidebook produced by CADW for the full story. Armed with this you can then do what I did and troop dutifully around its ruined buildings to get some sense of how this castle came to be and how it was used by the aristos descended from the Norman settlers. One of its main subsequent uses was as a prison and it's with two of its more illustrious prisoners that I want to spend some time now.

Bishop Jeremy Taylor was a casualty of the religious and civil ferments that brought about the Civil War and the coming of Oliver Cromwell. A clergyman from the age of twenty, Jeremy Taylor was renowned for giving exceedingly good sermons (a bit like Mr Kipling's exceedingly good cakes!), which included bon mots such as:

It is impossible to make people understand their ignorance; for it requires knowledge to perceive it and therefore he that can perceive it hath it not.

and:

Mistake not. Those pleasures are not pleasures that trouble the quiet and tranquillity of thy life.

It's almost in the David Beckham league, isn't it?

Anyway, Jeremy rose to become chaplain firstly to Archbishop "Laudy, Laudy, Miss Clawdie" Laud and then to Charles I. Big mistake, because Charles I had his head chopped off soon afterwards and Taylor was imprisoned in Chepstow Castle. He was imprisoned there on two separate occasions, though when finally the monarchy was restored he was released and made a bishop in Ireland. He wasn't overfond of Guinness or soda bread, though, unsurprising given his strong Protestant views and he died there at the comparatively young (for a vicar) age of fifty-four.

Curiously enough, he was followed into prison in Chepstow Castle by someone whose political views he could not have been more opposed to - the famous regicide Henry Marten. Now I'm particularly drawn towards this character because my very first published book was a detective novel about the murder of a Registered Inspector (known as a Reggie) in the middle of a school inspection and I wanted to call it *Reggiecide* but in the end decided it was too obscure a reference. But Henry Marten is not that obscure. He was known in his early days as a bit of a lad where the ladies were concerned - " a great lover of pretty girls" is how John Aubrey describes him in his *Brief Lives*. Indeed it is because of this trait that he allegedly came to dislike the king. Here's Aubrey's account of the story:

King Charles had a complaint against him for his wenching. It happened that Henry was in Hyde Park one time when his Majesty was there, going to see a race. The King espied him, and said aloud: 'Let that ugly rascal be gone out of the park, that whoremaster, or else 1 will not see the sport.' ... So Henry went away patiently, but it lay stored up deep in his heart. ... He was as far from a Puritan as light from darkness but shortly after he was chosen Knight of the Shire [i.e. elected as MP] ... and proved a deadly enemy to the King.

Deadly enemy indeed! Henry Marten squandered his family wealth on the Parliamentarian cause and slagged off the very idea of royalty. He played a leading role in the trial of the king, drafting the original charges against him, and was one of the signatories to Charles I's death warrant. In fact he and Cromwell flicked ink at one another at the signing. He later fell out with Cromwell and then his wild ways and casual approach to money led him into bankruptcy. When Charles II was restored to the monarchy, Henry Marten was tried and inevitably found guilty of regicide, for which crime he was sentenced to life imprisonment at Chepstow. Here, in what is now known as Marten's Tower, he spent the last

12 years of his life in not uncomfortable circumstances. He had his own servants, was allowed to receive visitors and even to call on neighbouring gentry.

It sounds not unlike the prison regime that our own dearly beloved Lord Archer has enjoyed in more recent times.

Early in 2003, Michael Hancocks, a leading light in the Aston Manor Brewery in Birmingham, admitted trying to lace the drink known as Strongbow cider, produced by the long-established Bulmer's. Aston Manor makes Frosty Jack cider and Hancocks (like Blackadder's faithful sidekick Baldrick) had devised a cunning plot to steal a march on his rivals, employing a chemist to create a contaminant which could be dropped into the Bulmer's vats and poison them. Unfortunately for Hancocks, the Bulmer's employee he had sought to bribe informed the police and he was arrested before any of the contaminated yeast was used. In any case, the contaminant, when tested, proved not to be as strong as Hancocks had hoped. Even if it had found its way into the Bulmer's cider-making operation, all it would have done is caused diarrhoea - something which some of the cider-drinkers I see hanging around park benches are undoubtedly familiar with anyway.

Bulmer's Strongow takes its name from the legendary Richard "Strongbow" de Clare, another of the top dog Norman knights. Richard's father Gilbert de Clare, also sometimes known as "Strongbow" (pay attention at the back - there's a test later), was given the title of Lord of Striguil (the old name for Chepstow) by King Stephen in 1138 - a title Richard inherited ten years later. As was the way in those days (what do I mean 'those days'? Just think of Geoffrey Howe's assassination of Maggie Thatcher or Clare Short's hatchet job on Tony Blair), those in power fell out from time to time and Richard was not in favour with Henry II when he came to the throne. So, being out of favour and also a bit short of cash, Strongbow took up the offer to assist Dermot MacMurchada, king of Leinster, to regain the Irish throne, tempted no doubt also by the bonus of getting Dermot's lovely daughter Aoife as his wife. For the rest of his life Strongbow was in Ireland, either fighting the Paddies or governing them from Dublin.

Gerald of Wales described Strongbow as a tall man with red hair, freckles, grey eyes and a soft voice:

> *"In war Strongbow was more of a leader than a soldier... When he took-up his position in the midst of battle, he stood firm as an immovable standard around which his men could re-group and take refuge. In war he remained steadfast and reliable in good fortune and bad alike. . .."*

Richard de Clare, Strongbow, lord of Striguil and one-time occupier of Chepstow Castle, died in 1176 but will forever be associated with the Anglo-Norman insurgence into Ireland, for his initial forays were rapidly followed by those of Henry II himself and the whole sorry story of the English exploitation of Ireland goes back to those days.

I began this chapter with mention of *Blazing Saddles* and end it with mention of racing saddles. For Chepstow Racecourse, ironically in the parkland that once belonged to Nathaniel Wells's Piercefield House, is known throughout the land for being the site where the Welsh Grand National is held every year. Britain's youngest racecourse, opened only in 1926, stages racing throughout the year, on the flat and over the jumps. Two of the winners of the Welsh Grand National, Rag Trade and Corbière, have gone on to win the Grand National proper at Aintree Racecourse in the same year, and two other winners, Burrough Hill Lad and Master Oats, went on to win that other prestigious long-distance race, the Cheltenham Gold Cup.

Highlights of the flat racing include Frankie Dettori becoming the first teenager since Lester Piggott to ride 100 winners in a season in 1990; Pat Eddery becoming the first jockey for 38 years to ride 200 winners in one season; and the world record set by Sir Gordon Richards when he rode 11 consecutive winners at a two-day meeting back in 1933.

But the greatest event in the history of Chepstow Racecourse has to be the Mascots Race of 2001. Those of you who attend major football matches will be familiar with the trend in recent years for each club to acquire a mascot, who dresses up in a silly costume and performs daft tricks as part of the pre-match entertainment. Now these are all supposed to be part of the general fun but occasionally mascots can take their role a little too seriously. Cyril the Swan of Swansea once ripped the head off Millwall's Zampa the Lion and dropkicked it into the crowd. Robbie the Bobby, Bury's mascot, was sent off for ripping the ears off Peterborough's rabbit mascot. The most-publicised instance was when Wolfie, I'm sad to say the mascot of my own much-loved Wolverhampton Wanderers, started a fight with all three of Bristol City's Three Little Pigs. Shortly afterwards he lost his position with the Wolves which led him to reflect on his life and times thus:

"I'm a signwriter. Eighty per cent of my time I write things like 'Pork chops 99p lb' and every time I have those pigs in my mind. It's going to live with me forever. I deal with butchers on a regular basis. Ironic really, isn't it?"

The 2001 Mascots Race featured one of the above, though not, alas, Wolfie. The line up was as follows:

1. Cyril the Swan (Swansea City FC)
2. Fergal the Shark (Swansea RFC)
3. Captain Gas (Bristol Rovers FC)
4. Ronny the Raven (Bridgend RFC)
7. Dino the Dragon (Glamorgan County Cricket Club)
8. Bartly the Bluebird (Cardiff City FC)
9. Jack the Slip (Jack Brown Bookmakers)
11. Harry the Hawk (Hampshire County Cricket Club)
12. Kingsley Royal Lion (Reading Football Club)
13. Freddy the Fox (Heatherton County Sports Park)
14. Spytty the Dog (Newport FC)
15. Dyfrig the Dragon (Chepstow Racecourse)
16. Funky Fledgling (Swindon Town FC)

According to contemporary reports, the race was a humdinger, though it is alleged that Cyril the Swan started fighting before the race proper began. He claimed he had merely stumbled. However, it was not much of a race because Freddy the Fox was well ahead after a short distance and never relinquished that lead.

I understand that representations are currently being made to the International Olympic Committee to have Mascot Racing officially entered into the next but one Olympic Games. At present, there is no doubt that Britain has the outstanding competitors in this rapidly growing sport and I'm all for its inclusion.

But please, don't tell the Yanks about it - they're sure to start dressing up and training for the event and then they'll do what they do with virtually every other sport and win all the medals. Mind you, on second thoughts, they don't need to do the dressing up bit - they could simply send Michael Jackson.

3 Chepstow to Monmouth

In the short period of time I had in Chepstow that sultry Sunday evening, I walked the first mile or so of the Offa's Dyke Path from Sedbury Cliffs back into the town. A boulder marks the start of the path and just below it you can walk down to the edge of the Severn Estuary and gaze in awe at that wonder of the modern age, the Severn Bridge, which takes traffic in and out of Wales. I was amazed to find the Dyke itself so clearly evident on this short stretch, even though the guidebook had indicated as much. It was my first walk on this very special earthwork and I was truly humbled from the beginning that it should have survived so long in such a good condition. Ditch and bank are clearly in evidence for a good quarter of a mile.

After dodging the beaten-up Ford Escorts driven by baseball-capped youths with tattoos and loud drum n' bass blasting through their open windows whose idea of fun it was to race around Chepstow's narrow streets looking for potential suicide-seekers, I had then found respite in the CAMRA-recommended Coach and Horses, where I had a pleasant pint of Brains Reverend James bitter. Then, after ditching my boots, I walked downtown to the Boat Inn by the riverside. Here I enjoyed an excellent meal of steak, strawberries and cream, followed by Irish coffee, at the same time as gazing below me at the chocolate-brown River Wye that swirled past and wondering about George Borrow's claim that he had supped from this murky water on his tour through Wales. What kind of stomach did George have? On the tall limestone cliffs opposite the Boat Inn, where England begins and Wales ends, someone has painted a Union Jack flag, presumably as a statement of some sort. Very sad, really.

Borrow's journey through Wales, described in his classic *Wild*

Wales, ended in Chepstow, where the writer, after supping from the River Wye, returned to his inn for dinner and:

> *"I called for a bottle of port, and placing my feet against the*
> *sides of the grate I passed my time drinking wine and singing*
> *Welsh songs till ten o'clock at night..."*

I returned to my lodging, not to sing Welsh songs but reflecting on this introduction to the border country that I was to be following for all of my journey, for the Offa's Dyke Path dodges in and out of England and Wales throughout its length. Would I find other signs of national pride and prejudice? Time would tell.

Next day I was off early, the weather still hot and humid, despite overnight thunderstorms. Just a mile or so out of Chepstow you come out on top of some limestone cliffs where there's a spot known as Wintour's Leap and old Johnny Wintour was an interesting cove who you might be interested to learn more about.

Sir John Wintour, to give him his proper title, lived in the family property of Whitecross Manor in Lydney at the time of the Civil War. This Johnny was a fervent Royalist but, unlike nearby Chepstow which stayed loyal to the king throughout, Gloucester was much more sympathetic to the Parliamentarian cause. The Wintours owned extensive territory in the Forest of Dean, including an ironworks, and Johnny's blatant support for the Royalist cause led to a number of ding-dongs, during one of which his wife Mary beat off an attack on Whitecross Manor by the Parliamentarian commander of Gloucester, presumably by throwing saucepans at him. Eventually, Wintour was no longer able to keep the hordes at bay and, rather than surrender, he set fire to the manor and set off on horseback in the direction of the River Wye. There, on the 200 foot high cliffs, Cromwell's troops thought they had him cornered but he drove his horse over the cliff, shouting "Go, Johnny, go, go, go!", and landed safely down below on the river bank, where a Royalist ship was waiting to transport him to France. Hence Wintour's Leap. It's a good story, though it's more likely that he knew some secret pathways down the rock face of which his pursuers were unaware.

In 1649 Wintour, back in England, was imprisoned in the Tower of London but he must have been a crafty so-and-so because by 1652 his fortunes had so improved that he was allowed to buy back his lands from the Parliamentary Commissioners and he built a new ironworks in the grounds of his former home. After the restoration of the monarchy, his lot improved even further and Samuel Pepys records meeting him thus:

"Up by 4 or 5 o'clock and to the office and there draw up an agreement between the King and Sir John Wintour about the Forest of Dean: and having done it, he came himself, whom I observed be a man of fine parts; and we read it, and both liked it well."

Presumably they both went off for a spot of wenching, which appears from Pepys's diaries to have been the major pastime in England before football was invented. By 1663 Johnny had re-established control over the whole area and was employing 500 woodcutters in the Forest of Dean, which brought him further trouble for over-cutting timber. He died in 1687, no doubt still shouting "Go, Johnny, go, go, go!" as he set off for the pearly gates.

Nowadays Wintour's Leap is more familiar to rock climbers for whom it provides exciting challenges and the opportunity to use a strange language, which is almost as impenetrable as that of skateboarders. Here's a typical example from a bloke who climbed on the Wintour's Leap rocks not so long ago:

"I got some gear in behind her and this was now full-on commitment. It was great! Hands, feet, laybacking, jamming, crimping everything! I even managed a frontal mounting job which got the ground control pretty excited and the team mood was on a definite high as associations of the opposite sex were inevitable."

Full frontal mounting, eh! I suspect old Johnny Wintour would have approved of that, especially as he was a man of fine parts. But who knows?

Tintern Abbey nestles in a loop of the River Wye a few miles further upstream and just off the Offa's Dyke Path, which passes through some very old forestation on its way there as well as another well-preserved section of the actual Dyke. You first see the magnificent shell of Tintern from a huge grey limestone crag that towers above in the cliffs. This crag is known as the Devil's Pulpit because the devil is supposed to have spent much of his time there shouting obscenities, presumably Anglo-Saxon ones, at the monks in the abbey down below and tempting them with untold riches.

> *"Come on, you f***ing monks! Wouldn't you rather be driving round in a Roller and eating caviare than sitting on your canticles all day and night?"*

It must have been difficult to resist.

Now Tintern owes its fame to the fact that Wordsworth composed a poem here and Turner painted its haunting buildings. I'll come to those two later but Tintern's origins lie in the fact that it was the place where, after a long reign, the Ancient British king Tewdrig chose to end his life as a hermit. Sadly for him, the Saxon raiders were getting closer and he was forced one more time to take up arms, which he did, winning a massive battle at Tintern where the Wye can be forded. Tewdrig himself, however, was mortally wounded and, although his wounds were washed in a nearby spring of fresh water that miraculously appeared from the ground, he died at nearby Mathern, whose name means 'martyred king.'

Altogether now, aah!

The French monks who chose this place for their monastery in 1131 were initially noted for their poverty but, as with so many religious orders, they couldn't resist the lure of lolly, maybe because Satan was himself tempting them from the nearby Devil's Pulpit. Tintern Abbey became one of the richest monasteries in the land, holding over 3000 acres of land and driving the local Gwent peasants off the common land with their extensive flocks of sheep. Its demise came with Henry VIII's dissolution of the monasteries in 1539 but before that occurred it was the home for a while of a pilgrim who was fed up with the evils of society. On joining the order he was required to take a vow of silence and was only allowed to speak two words each year.

He took the vow and began his first year of service without saying a word. At the end of one long year he was brought before the head of the monastery and was asked what two words he would like to say.

His response was: "Food bad."

And that was it for another long year, until he was once again allowed to say another two words. After two years of service he was brought before the head of the monastery and was asked what two words he would like to say.

His response was: "More blankets."

And that was it for another long year, until he was once again allowed to say another two words. After three years of service he was brought before the head of the monastery and asked what two words he would like to say.

His response was: "I quit!"

The head monk answered back, "You might as well. You've done nothing but complain since you've been here!"

Now I don't know if William Wordsworth or Turner had heard about this. They came to Tintern because it was on the romantic Wye - a river whose picturesque sights had made it a favourite tourist haunt in the eighteenth and early nineteenth centuries. Turner painted it in typical Turner fashion while Wordsworth's poem, simply entitled *Lines composed a few miles above Tintern Abbey*, was written in 1798 and appeared as the final poem in the revolutionary *Lyrical Ballads*. Here's how it starts:

Five years have passed; five summers, with the length
Of five long winters! And again I hear

These waters, rolling from their mountain-springs
With a soft inland murmur. - Once again
Do I behold these steep and lofty cliffs,
That on a wild secluded scene impress
Thoughts of more deep seclusion; and connect
The landscape with the quiet of the sky.

Wordsworth was a great walker. It was nothing for him to walk twenty miles a day, just for the hell of it. While he walked, frequently he was composing poetry, often spouting it out loud whether anyone was passing or not. If you didn't want to hear this, it was best to look down where your eyes would inevitably have focused on his legs, described by his friend Thomas de Quincey thus:

"He was, upon the whole, not a well made man. His legs were pointedly condemned by all female connoisseurs in legs; not that they were bad in any way which would force itself upon your notice - there was no absolute deformity about them; and undoubtedly they had been serviceable legs beyond the average standard of human requisition; for I calculate, upon good data, that with these identical legs Wordsworth must have traversed a distance of 175,000 to 180,000 English miles - a mode of exercise which, to him, stood in the stead of alcohol and other stimulants; to which indeed he was indebted for a life of unclouded happiness, and we for much of what is excellent in his writings."

Didn't they write long sentences in those days? My grammar checker's going wild.

This particular poem stemmed from the poet's second visit to the ruins of Tintern Abbey, the first having taken place in 1793 when he was full of hope for the new French Republic. Five years later, now sharing a home in the Lake District with his sister Dorothy (we won't go into that here!), he and his sister had spent time with Coleridge and gone on a four-day ramble to the Wye valley. The poem is a very long reflection on memory.

So long, in fact, that no one ever quotes any more than those first few lines. The rest is forgotten.

Just upriver of Tintern is the tiny village of Brockweir, which is home to an attractive Moravian church with Gothic windows, Art Nouveau glass and a bellcote. Now when I first read about a Moravian church, I had visions of some Dr Frankenstein type having sailed up the Wye and planted his community here, rather like the French monks had planted themselves at Tintern or the Jehovah's Witnesses have planted themselves just about everywhere. The truth is a little stranger.

In the same period that Wordsworth was tramping around on his unattractive legs and spouting his lofty odes, Brockweir was a small shipbuilding community of about 350 people. It's hard to believe nowadays, but some pretty big ships were built here, not just trows and river boats but ocean-going schooners like the 506-ton Constantine launched in 1847. Apart from building ships, these people spent their time getting wrecked in the seven pubs that were in the community or gambling on cockfights. Brockweir was famous for being "a city of refuge for persons of desperate and lawless character". Not the sort of community, you would have thought, to welcome a missionary from Bristol representing the church of Moravia. However, the Rev. Ramftler (not quite Dr Frankenstein) seems to have been remarkably convincing for in a fairly short time he had persuaded the locals to build a church on what had previously been the cock pit and to give up their lascivious ways.

There is a graveyard next to the church, which holds, among many others, the remains of one Flora Klickmann who has the distinction of being the first female editor in England. The magazine she edited from 1908 to 1930 was called *The Girls Own Paper and Woman's Magazine*. The magazine began life in 1880 and its typical contents were two long stories, a short story, three poems, an article on the 'Girlhood of Queen Victoria', an article on 'Fashionable Costumes of Long Ago', articles on needlework and cookery, 'Useful Hints', and a Competition which asked girls to write 'an essay on the life of any one famous English woman, born in the present century'. Its proclaimed aim as a magazine was "to foster and develop that which was highest and noblest in the girlhood and womanhood of England" and Flora Klickman continued this tradition throughout her time as editor.

I suppose the modern equivalent would be magazines like *Sugar*, apparently Britain's No. 1 Girls' Mag, which includes articles on anorexia, rape and epilepsy as well as advice on fashion ("be a babe in black 'n' white") and beauty ("smouldering looks for when the sun goes down"). It also has the latest on 'Top Celebs' ("see what the stars get from the supermarket" and "The J.Lo-down"), together with vast amounts of advice about boys and how to attract them ("be first-time flirt fantastic", "fellas say why they'd fall for you" and a special Love Quiz Book).

Plus ça change, eh?

There is only one pub in Brockweir nowadays. It's called the Brockweir Country Inn and it advertises itself as serving Hook Norton beer. Much as I like this particular beer, it was only eleven in the morning as I went through the village and it was far too early for me to conduct research in this pub. It also saved me the potential embarrassment, which had happened to me once before, of going to the bar and requesting from the barmaid (it always is a barmaid on such occasions);

"Half of Hook, please."

You have to say it quickly to get my meaning but, trust me, it is a phrase you should always be very careful about using.

I was feeling strong on this first day, so pressed on along the Offa's Dyke Path, taking the alternative route through green lanes and minor tracks across St Briavel's Common in preference to the Wyeside walk, and was soon in Bigsweir, which is the highest tidal point on the River Wye. Then it was back into woodland, this time through Highbury Woods which is maintained by English Nature and where I swore I heard a nuthatch as I was walking.

The nearby St Briavel's Castle, nowadays used most imaginatively as a Youth Hostel, dates back to the twelfth century.

As well as being one of that chain of border castles thrown up by the Anglo-Norman aristos, St Briavel's served as the administrative headquarters for the Royal Hunting Forest, better known to you and me as the Forest of Dean - that unique geographical area between the River Wye and the River Severn. The Norman kings had been using the Forest as their private huntin', shootin' and fishin' grounds for quite some time before the castle was built - William's commissioning of the Domesday Book at Christmas 1086 took place at Gloucester because he was there for the hunting season. The Forest of Dean, however, had been the site of important human activity long before this.

There has been mining in the Forest since time immemorial. The Celts were followed by the Romans and later by the Normans. What were they mining? Coal certainly but just as importantly iron ore. And the wood of the Forest has been used over the centuries to produce charcoal and its oak is famous for providing the timber for the ships sailed by Drake, Raleigh and Nelson. The people of the Forest of Dean have always seen themselves as a race apart and all those born outside the Forest are regarded as foreigners. They also have a peculiarly self-mocking and wry sense of humour, as you'll see in this dialect story from there concerning the archetypal hero of the Forest, Jolter.

"I cosn't git me donk under this bridge. 'Is yurs be too 'igh," complained Jolter.

"Dig a little trench under the bridge, Jolter," advised his friend.

Jolter, amazed at such a foolish idea, retorted: "Thee gurt sawney vool, 'tes the donk's yurs what be too 'igh, not 'is veet."

The most famous person to come from the Forest of Dean was television playwright Dennis Potter, the son of a Forest miner, whose merging of fantasy and reality in his plays established new ways of using the medium. Some of that fantasy, particularly in the sexually explicit scenes, earned him the title of "TV's Mr. Filth" from the popular press but his work, especially *The Singing Detective, Pennies from Heaven* and *The Blue Remembered Hills*, created a legacy of outstanding television. I vividly remember the 1979 *Blue Remembered Hills* with its cast of adults dressed in children's clothes and enacting their childish emotions and responses. It was brilliant. Whatever you think of Potter, you could not accuse him of pandering to popular taste. His TV dramas were challenging and original but spoke to everyone. Can you imagine a new Dennis Potter trying to find space on the thousand channels that we now have, all filled with makeover shows and reality TV?

Jolter would no doubt have had a view on Dennis Potter but I had to get on and by two o'clock I had reached Redbrook and called in at The Boat Inn just across the footbridge next to the dead railway over the Wye. The hot weather had brought out the usual babes in their cropped T-shirts, showing off their latest tattoos at the base of their spines, plus a few locals who were there to cool off. I do recommend The Boat - it's got lovely old stone flags for its floor, a variety of furnishings (none of your standard repro. stuff here), a cheery landlord who shouts "Sack the juggler!" whenever a plate breaks, real ales and an interesting menu. I was tempted by the Pan Haggerty Plain or Bacon, described as "a Scottish dish made with repeated layers of potatoes, onions, garlic and cheese, even more delicious when served with bacon" but settled on a tuna baguette. This turned out to be so massive that I was forced to order a second pint of Freeminer's Speculation Ale to wash it down. What a name for a beer! What a hard life!

Unsurprisingly, I don't have much recall of the next part of the day's walk but I know that it was only a couple of miles of hillside walking until I emerged in the grounds of The Kymin. The unusual buildings here owe their origins to their siting, from which there are amazing views over several counties. A toposcope on the hillside overlooking Monmouth points you towards Sugar Loaf near Abergavenny, the Brecon Beacons, Hatterall Ridge which I would be traversing in a couple of days, and The Skirrid. It has always been a favourite picnic place for the people of

Monmouth, none more so than the eighteenth century toffs of the town who met here every Tuesday for *al fresco* lunches and, no doubt, a spot of serious tippling. However, the weather then was as unpredictable as it is now and in 1794 they clubbed together to build the banqueting house known as the Roundhouse that is now managed by the National Trust.

A few years later the Naval Temple was built as a monument to several British admirals who had won decisive battles and smashed the navies of France or Spain or wherever in the seventeenth and eighteenth centuries. Amongst those so praised was Admiral Horatio Nelson, who came to visit The Kymin in the company of his mistress Lady Hamilton and her husband.

On the steep climb down from The Kymin into Monmouth, I came upon a pair of black female knickers. Might Horatio have ripped them off Lady H. in his hot-blooded fervour? I wondered. Even a one-armed man can achieve wondrous things. Speculating thus, I crossed the old bridge over the River Wye and entered the ancient town of Monmouth.

That evening in Monmouth I visited the CAMRA-recommended Green Dragon pub, whose clientèle were all male, all swearing and all well on the way to being drunk by 6.30 in the evening. A sign above its bar announced: "This bar is dedicated to those souls of other days, who made drinking a pleasure and achieved contentment long before capacity, who, whatever they drank, enjoyed it and remained...GENTLEMEN!" Oh yes, I thought, looking back at the assembly as I left. Some chance.

So I dined in the King's Head hotel in Agincourt Square, which is now a Wetherspoon's pub. Here I was refreshed by decent beer (Jennings's Cocker Hoop, since you ask), reasonable food and a pleasant music-free atmosphere.

"What's your most popular beer?" I asked the barman there.

"Hook Norton, when we have it," he explained. "It goes very quickly."

"I bet you have to be careful how you answer when someone asks for half of Hook," I said, grinning salaciously.

"They usually drink pints here," he replied, clearly missing my point completely. "I can't recall anyone ever asking for a half."

"No, you have to say it very fast," I tried to explain, rather lamely. "You know, half-of-Hook."

He smiled at me as if I was some kind of blithering idiot that he had to tolerate. I suppose it was part of his training. I guess the local Further Education college must have a GNVQ course in bartending, including How to Serve a Full Pint, How to Stand at the Opposite End of the Bar to Where the Customers are, and How to Smile at Irritating Punters.

"I suppose you'd really be in trouble if they asked for a full one," I continued, pushing this feeble witticism well beyond its limits.

"As I say, sir," he replied patiently, "our customers usually ask for pints."

He hadn't got it. And I wasn't going to help him understand. So I left and wondered down to the riverside to listen to the birds singing in the balmy summer's evening before returning via the underpass of the main road where I read:

IVAN HAS A SMALL WEENER.

And underneath:

"WE AGREE". THE GIRLS OF MONMOUTH GIRLS' SCHOOL.

Bet they hadn't been reading *The Girls Own Paper and Woman's Magazine*.

4 Monmouth

I just couldn't help thinking, as I entered the historic town of Monmouth, of Laurence Olivier on the battlefield at Agincourt urging his weary troops on with those immortal words:

Once more unto the breach, dear friends, once more;
Or close the wall up with our English dead!

And it's no accident that I should think thus, for the town's central square is called Agincourt Square after the great battle against the French fought and won by the town's greatest son, and some would argue England's finest king, Henry V.

Henry was born in Monmouth Castle in 1388, the son of Henry IV (Parts 1 and 2) and Mary Bohun. Known as Prince Hal, by the age of sixteen he was already considered to be an accomplished soldier and led the English army against the Percy uprising at the Battle of Shrewsbury. Aged eighteen he routed the forces of Glendower, thus bringing Wales under English subjection and recruiting the Gwent longbowmen into the English army. On his accession to the crown in 1413, he was already a battle-hardened veteran and, after putting down a Lollard rebellion led by Sir John Oldcastle (allegedly the model for Shakespeare's Sir John Falstaff) and survived an assassination plot devised by nobles still loyal to Richard II, he felt confident to take on the might of France.

In 1415 he proposed to marry Catherine, daughter of the French king Charles VI, requesting the old Plantagenet lands of Normandy and Anjou as his dowry. When Charles said 'No way, José', Henry declared war and invaded France, defeating the mighty French army at Agincourt, largely thanks to the Welsh longbowmen whose arrows mowed down the French soldiers from afar and introduced a new and fearsome weapon to the armoury of war. By 1419 Henry had captured large swathes of France and, after Charles VI had signed a peace treaty, he at last married Catherine in 1420. One year later the only son of that marriage was born but Henry died soon after, never having seen this son.

Well, that's the official story, as recorded by medieval historians, as wonderfully gilded by Shakespeare in that patriotic play with the same name as our English hero, and as portrayed by Olivier (and more recently by Kenneth Branagh) in the film version of Shakespeare's famous play. But does it stand up?

No, of course it doesn't. We like our myths, don't we? And we need to have our heroes and heroines, bestriding their times and ours with their mighty deeds. And I'm quite certain that Olivier's portrayal of the warrior king leading his underdog forces against the mighty enemy was important in sustaining the plucky little Brit myth as the Second World War drew to its close. But the truth of Henry V is a little different from the picture that Shakespeare chose to give us. First of all, Henry was a serial betrayer of his friends. The Percies, father Thomas and son Harry, a.k.a. Hotspur, had been his chums in earlier years and had advised him on military and political matters. That didn't stop the young Prince Hal from turning on them and defeating them at the Battle of Shrewsbury, nor from displaying the quartered body of the slain Hotspur in Newcastle, London, Chester and York. Sir John Oldcastle, too, had been a companion in battle with whom Henry later fell out and had executed.

As for his claim to lands in France, well this was a sort of traditional call made by English kings ever since the arrival of their Norman forebears in 1066. It was a bit like the Argentinians claiming the Falkland Isles as their own, or the Spanish wanting Gibraltar back. If you want to show you're hard, you have to demand the restoration of old lands, even though you have no real right to them. So Henry set off for France, probably just to do a bit of plundering before scooting back home. But then he had the most tremendous good fortune. The French army, heavily armed and ready for a traditional ding-dong in which they would have outnumbered the English invading force, got stuck in the mud, while the English (or rather the Welsh) longbowmen stuck up their two fingers at the French, placed successive arrows between those fingers, and settled the battle. The English have been putting two fingers up to the French ever since.

Mind you, we also put two fingers up to the Germans, the Dutch, the Americans, the Greeks, the Russians, the Italians, in fact anybody we don't like. The V-sign has become a signal in British culture that indicates contempt for the person or persons to whom it is made and its origin lies at Agincourt. I have heard it said that the sign really means "Pluck yew!", being the taunt of the bowmen whose weapons were traditionally made from the wood of the yew tree. Can you believe that? Not plucking likely! Anyway, after the battle, Henry showed his unpleasant nature once again when he broke the rules of the Geneva Convention and ordered his troops to kill any French injured soldiers lying on the battlefield.

So, as you stand in the rather fine Agincourt Square beneath the statue of Henry or wander around the ruins of Monmouth Castle where he was born, just think of the myths that history has created and which still guide our lives in so many ways and:

Cry "God for Harry! England and Saint George!"

But don't give the Monmouth citizenry the V-sign or you'll be in deep doo-doo!

The recently appointed Archbishop of Canterbury, Rowan Williams, was Bishop of Monmouth a decade ago and in those days his hopes of promotion looked bleak, because of some of the views that he openly espoused. He is in favour, for instance, of women priests, of accepting homosexuality both within the church and within the laity, and of allowing divorced people to remarry in church. He got the tag of "troublesome priest" - a phrase used originally by Henry II about Thomas á Becket. Remarkably, it seems now, some of these views are perceived to be much more mainstream and the views of those who disagree with Williams are seen to be reactionary.

I don't know how much or how little time Rowan Williams spent in Monmouth any more than I, or anyone else for that matter, knows how much or how little his distinguished ecclesiastic predecessor Geoffrey of Monmouth spent here. But Geoffrey is single-handedly responsible for handing down to us some of the greatest myths of our history and, since he took his name from this town, we must presume that he had some relationship with it, probably that he was born in the area. What is known from old records is that between 1129 and 1151 he was at a religious house in Oxford, that he was appointed Bishop of St Asaph in 1152 and that he died in 1155. And the historical myths for which he was responsible? They are in a Geoffrey's *History of the Kings of Britain*, in which he traces our nation's origins back to one Brutus, the great-grandson of Aeneas, who leads his people out of Greece to the island of Albion, which is renamed Britain after him and where he becomes its first king, roughly 1100 years before the birth of Christ.

The story continues through a succession of kings, most of whose names are instantly forgettable, though we do meet for the first time Leir, whom Shakespeare's turned into King Lear, and Coel, who is better known as the nursery rhyme's Old King Cole ("with his pipe and his bowl"). The latter half of the book is taken up with Geoffrey's loving accounts of the deeds of King Arthur, which formed the basis of the legend of Camelot that exists in most people's minds to this day. Geoffrey's *History* ended in 689 and amazingly became the accepted truth about British history for the best part of six hundred years. Why? Because it pandered to the desires of the new aristocracy, the French robber barons who were in reality little more than plundering bullies, to belong to an ancient dynasty - one that linked the Welsh and the French and one that was the historical equivalent of Greece or Rome.

Presumably Geoffrey knew that his writing would have this effect and presumably also this was one of his main reasons for writing it. Where he got his stories from, no one knows. He himself says that they came from a book given to him by Walter,

Archdeacon of Oxford, but no trace of this book has been found and no other writer of that or later periods makes mention of such a book. So did he make the stories up? Well, it's quite possible that some of the tales he tells are complete fabrications, written to satisfy that thirst that we all possess to believe that we come from ancient and honourable stock. If that's so, then Geoffrey wasn't the first nor would he be the last, as we shall see later in this narrative, to seek to create an ancestry with chutzpah.

Three hundred years after his death in what was then the Monmouth Priory an oriel window was constructed in his memory, known still as Geoffrey's Window, though the crafty old Welshman never looked out of it. Beneath the window are three gargoyles of a knight, an angel and a miller. These represent the military, ecclesiastic and commercial origins of Monmouth, though they might just as easily represent Geoffrey himself, for the *History of the British Kings* was really a military history, he was himself a cleric, and the book was a best seller making it a commercial success.

So does it matter that the book was and is a fabrication? Just ask yourself how important it is to believe that *The Odyssey* or *The Aeneid* are true. As I've said, we need our myths and certainly the legend of Arthur, first brought to life on the page here in Geoffrey's book has retained its hold on our imaginations for a long time and it will run through this narrative, since the Welsh borderland holds more than its fair share of Arthur's secrets in its bosom.

I like old Geoff. I think he adds to the colour of things. And he's not so posy as those two TV history men who are making so much cash right now - David Sharkey and Simon Sharma. So let's have a bit more mythtory in our history, eh?

Another Monmouth citizen certainly brought lots of colour to life. The family of Charles Stewart Rolls came from Monmouth and there is a statue of him in Agincourt Square, just beneath that of Henry V. Though he was known as "Dirty Rolls" and "Petrolls" during his Cambridge days, you'll know him better as part of that great hyphenated motor car manufacturer Rolls-Royce. Charles's life, though brief - he died at the age of 33 - throws an interesting light on the early twentieth century and in particular on the development of that scourge of the quiet countryside, the automobile.

Rolls developed early in his life a love for speed and while at Cambridge became a racing cyclist, for which he was awarded a half blue. In 1896 he bought his first motor car from Paris and brought it back to Cambridge, where it was the first ever car to be based there. Can you imagine that now? He then started racing automobiles and joined with other motor enthusiasts to break a law that forbade automobile travel at over 4mph. As a result of their act, a new speed limit of 12 mph was introduced which was two hundred per cent faster than had previously been allowed. In 1901 he won a 1000-mile reliability trial and two years later established a world record of 93 mph.

By this time Rolls had become a co-founder of the Automobile Club and was in the business of selling cars, which were mostly French. In 1904 he was introduced to Fredrick Henry Royce, an engineer and car builder who was just beginning to produce quality motors. The salesman and the engineer went for a spin in one of Royce's motors and, though coming from opposite ends of the social spectrum, they fell for each other. Well, metaphorically speaking, if you catch my drift. Hence the hyphen that was to join them inextricably forever. That same year Rolls-Royce was born and rapidly established itself at the forefront of the quality car market. The famous emblem, ever after seen on the front of Rollers and known as *The Spirit of Ecstasy* was designed by another colleague in the motor world and was intended to represent "speed with silence, absence of vibration and the mysterious harnessing of great energy". It was modelled, however, on the rather dishy secretary of the Automobile Club.

Rolls by this time had become interested in aviation, becoming a keen exponent of hot-air ballooning. When he met the Wright Brothers at the New York Motor Show where he was exhibiting Rolls-Royces, he found a new enthusiasm and in 1910 he purchased his first plane. That same year he completed the first two-way crossing of the English Channel in his plane but his triumph was short-lived. One month later his biplane broke up in mid-air in a strong wind and, although he was only twenty feet above ground, the fall broke Rolls's skull and he died instantly. The statue in Monmouth depicts him in his flying mode.

I will never own a Roller. I don't even aspire to owning a Roller. And I'm not a person who, in general, drools over motor cars. But I have to say that Rolls-Royce cars justify their position as being smart-looking objects. They're slick and sleek and, when I've sold a million copies of this book, I might just buy one.

"Kiss me, Hardy," has to be one of the most repeated sayings in British oral history, handed down through the generations with little but the barest understanding of whence it came or why it matters. Comedians through the years have used it in jest and there's even a song by Serge Gainsburg (a perfidious Frenchman) with it as its title.

Yes, we all know it was said by England's great seadog, Admiral Horatio Nelson, as he lay dying on board his ship *Victory* at the Battle of Trafalgar when the perfidious ('cos they always are) French of Napoleon were defeated once and for all. But who was Hardy? And why was Nelson engaging in this final act of homoeroticism? And above all what's this story doing in this chapter?

Time for some explanations, methinks.

First of all, you need to know that there is a Nelson Museum in Monmouth and that the contents of this fine museum - personal effects of the naval hero, letters to Lady Hamilton, and other fascinating memorabilia - owe their origin to the collection of Lady Llangattock whose home was nearby. Lady L, who was also as it happens the mother of Charles Rolls, developed a fascination for Nelson for reasons that no one knows and spent her life collecting everything she could connected with the great hero. She bequeathed her collection to the town and they have been here ever since.

Now Horatio Nelson was born in Norfolk some two hundred and

fifty miles away and his links with Monmouth are rather tenuous to say the least. He visited the town in 1802 in the company of Emma, Lady Hamilton, and Lord Hamilton. Apparently Nelson gave approval to the Naval Temple next to The Kymin which is of course on the Offa's Dyke path. The trio picnicked there, as thousands have done before and since. By this time Nelson and Emma were openly lovers, an arrangement that was known about and presumably approved of by her husband. The two lovers had first met in Naples where she had been sent by her first partner to marry the much older Lord Hamilton in return for the repayment of a financial debt. Nelson, in Naples to gather reinforcements against the French, was already married but that never stopped a sailor, did it? Though he continued to provide for his wife Fanny financially, he shut her out emotionally. When she wrote in 1800, "Do, my dear husband, let us live together," he sent back the envelope inscribed, "Opened by mistake."

The relationship between the highly respected Admiral Nelson and Lady Hamilton was passionate and highly charged sexually, even though he was away at sea for large periods of time. She wrote to him daily, sometimes three or four times a day, and many of these letters were real rippers. You wonder how he managed to concentrate his energies on fighting sea battles. The affair scandalised polite society, partly because of the *mores* of the day but largely, I suspect, because Emma was low born, being the daughter of an illiterate blacksmith and had been mistress to two men before the marriage to Lord Hamilton.

On one occasion, when he returned to Naples from battle with his one arm shot away, despite having her husband living in the same house, Emma nursed Nelson with asses' milk and sought to cheer him up him with her dancing. I don't know what he thought of her dancing but I understand she never wore underwear as she thought it too uncomfortable, so I guess Nelson would have been immensely cheered up (and the knickers I found coming down from The Kymin couldn't have been hers, could they?). On the occasion of his fortieth birthday, she arranged a party with 1,800 guests. You could not accuse the pair of being indiscreet, could you?

So to October 1805 and the Battle of Trafalgar. Everyone, including Nelson and Napoleon, knew that this would be the decisive naval battle of their time. Success for Napoleon against the fleet of the Royal Navy and their one-armed Admiral would give him the key to the invasion of Britain and unlimited control of the world's seas. To Nelson fell the task of ensuring the survival of Britain as a separate entity from Europe (yes, I know, it's still causing us problems, isn't it?). Nelson may have been a bit of a bounder in his love life but as a naval commander he had no equal. His sailors trusted him implicitly and were ready to die for him. His innovative tactics for Trafalgar would ensure that many did but, because of their greater experience of such fighting, far less British died than French. The battle was decisively won, giving the British fleet command of the high seas for the next century during which time the British Empire spread across the globe.

But what of Horatio himself? Sadly he was hit by a single bullet, which shot through his backbone and his lungs rapidly began to fill with blood. He was taken below decks where he was attended by his chaplain, his surgeon and his colleague Admiral Hardy - yes, that's who it was! According to these witnesses, as he was close to death he said to Hardy:

"Take care of my dear Lady Hamilton, Hardy, take care of poor Lady Hamilton."

Then he paused and said very faintly:

"Kiss me, Hardy."

Hardy gave him a quick peck. Nelson then said:

"Now I am satisfied. Thank God I have done my duty."

And that was the end of Nelson and the end of this story, except to tell you that Lady Hamilton and their daughter Horatia were not looked after, not being invited to the great man's funeral and

41

receiving no pension. Emma Hamilton ended up in and out of the debtors' prison until she died at the age of forty-nine, a broken and ill woman.

Go and see the story told through the letters and memorabilia of the Nelson Museum in Monmouth. Then weep that yet another great English hero had feet of clay.

5 Monmouth to Hay-on-Wye

The next two days walking between Monmouth and Hay-on-Wye couldn't have been more different, though both cover roughly the same distance of 17 or so miles. The first day was a generally pleasant stroll through a rolling landscape along quiet lanes, across wheat-filled fields, through woody copses and old villages that have stood pretty much unchanged for centuries. The second day was an altogether different walk but I'll come to that later.

After leaving Monmouth through its old gatehouse on the bridge over the River Monmow which has been used for toll collection, as a guard room for the militia, as a bridewell, as a lock-up, as a store house and as a private dwelling at different times since its original erection in the 13th century, I was soon out in the country. It wasn't long before I met up with Martin, a heating engineer from Bradford-on-Avon, who was to be my frequent companion on the Offa's Dyke Path during the next few days.

We made good time on the early stretch, passing through the tiny settlement of Llanvihangel-Ystern-Llewern with its medieval church dedicated to St Michael of the Fiery Meteor (remember him in the bible?) and then some way further on the village of Llantilio Crossenny. There used to be a pub in this village named the Hostry Inn and many Offa's Dyke walkers would stop off there for refreshment midway between Monmouth and Pandy. Sadly, despite the resistance of the local population (who rarely went in there) and Mid-Wales CAMRA (who once voted it their pub of the year in the not-too-distant past), the Hostry Inn has closed its doors and has been converted by the previous landlord into a private dwelling. The Hostry Inn dates from 1459 and its sign used to include a memorial to Sir David Gam, who lived in the village. Gam was originally David Llewellyn but was renamed because of his pronounced squint and is the model for Shakespeare's Fluellen in *Henry V*, a comic knight who is the original stage Welshman with his leeks and his "Look you's". The real Sir David Gam did fight with Henry V at Agincourt, taking a band of archers with him (and presumably their V-signs), and was belatedly knighted on the battlefield as he lay dying.

Another couple of cross-country miles brought us to the remains of White Castle where Margaret and Sue, employees of CADW, guarded the kiosk which sold us tickets to enter for a rest from the sun and to eat our lunches.

"You get very busy here then?" I asked, after we had shelled out our cash. I could see two people in the castle grounds.

"Ooh, yes," replied Margaret. "Very busy. We never stop really. Lots of school parties. We've got two lots coming tomorrow, one from London and one from Coventry. Miles away really. They're all from England, mind, not from Wales. They say it's because castles are on the curriculum in England but not in Wales."

"Takes two of you to look after it then, does it?" I asked with a twinkle in my eye.

"Ooh, no," protested Margaret, "Sue's my boss."

"Just come to check up on Margaret then?" I queried.

"Ooh, no," said Sue. "I don't need to check up on Margaret. I've just come to see everything's alright really."

"And to have a cup of tea." I pointed to her mug.

"Well, you have to, don't you? It's so hot, isn't it? And you need something refreshing," Sue answered. "I'm based at Tintern actually. And this time of year it's always packed full of tourists, usually American. It's nice to get away occasionally. And I always like coming to see Margaret."

Well, you would, wouldn't you? In the middle of this lovely Welsh countryside, miles from anywhere, and guarding this almost perfect monument to the past.

The White Castle is so called because it was once literally covered in white plaster. Built by the Normans, possibly by our old friend William fitz "Ozzie" Osbern, the castle was extended at various times over the coming centuries as the French invaders sought to protect themselves more fully and to demonstrate their power over the local Welsh boyos. At one time White Castle was held by one Humphrey de Burgh (ancestor of Chris, of course) who was briefly stand-in regent for Henry III when he was still too young to reign and whose second wife was King John's ex-queen. Another occupant was allegedly the infamous "Black" William de Braose, who goes down in history as the man who invited the local Welsh chieftains to Abergavenny Castle one Christmas for a party with crackers and mince pies and everything and then promptly murdered them.

To see it now, surrounded by miles and miles of agricultural land, you'd find it hard to believe that it was ever necessary to build a castle here to ward off the Welsh but I suppose its main function really was rather like that of those more modern symbols of power, the Kremlin or the White House. Look at me, it is proclaiming brashly, if I can build something as grand as this, what can't I do to you? And I guess, just like today, these symbols worked. Or they did for several centuries until people had forgotten what all the fuss was about and just wanted to get on with their lives.

And we wanted to get on with our trek so, bidding Margaret and Sue farewell, we resumed our journey towards Pandy, which was to be the end-point of that day's walking. It was again steaming hot and when, three miles further on, we passed St Cadoc's church in Llangattock Lingoed and discovered that the Hunter's Moon Inn just beyond it was actually open, I allowed Martin to persuade me that we really needed to support the local economy by having a drink there. And so we did. And very refreshing it was too, so much so that I suggested another but Martin insisted we press on.

The 13th century St Cadoc's church was closed as we passed it, a notice informing us that its roof was being restored. It looked to me as if more than this was being restored, as the exterior of the building, with its unusual and attractive white plastering (I guess this must be a feature of the area), was also being renovated. I wrote later to the minister of the church, Reverend Jean Prosser, and found out more. And there was a fascinating understory as well.

Apparently it became obvious to the regular churchgoers (all four of them) that the roof was about to cave in, so they launched an appeal to save it. A Fork Supper brought in £5000, various church trusts coughed up a further £9000 but the big win was £200,000 from the Heritage Lottery. Then CADW offered to fund half of the building repairs and all seemed well. However, there was another complication - bats in the belfry. A colony of very rare Lesser Horseshoe bats had made their home in the church roof many years ago and the work had to be timed to coincide with their period of hibernation between October and April. According to Jean Prosser, work on the tower of the church was completed on time and the bats had returned to breed, assisted by extra insulation and a heater. Lucky bats!

Llangattock's most famous son is Sir Henry Morgan, the seventeenth century buccaneer, most famous for answering a query from one of the Spanish galleons he was approaching:

"Where's your buccaneers?"

with the timely response:

"On either side of me buckin' head."

Much of the story of Henry Morgan is shrouded in myth for his exploits were first told by a Dutch writer who had sailed with Morgan but whose version of events inevitably tended towards the more bloodthirsty end of things. Morgan's buccaneering took place in the Caribbean but we don't even know how he got there. One version says he was 'Barbados'd', i.e. beaten over the head on a dark Bristol night and thrown on board an ocean-going ship; another says he enlisted in the forces of General Venables (ancestor of the great Terry) and Vice-Admiral Penn (father of the man who named Pennsylvania), sent out by Cromwell in 1655 to sort out the Spanish in the Caribbean area. At any rate, it was in the Caribbean area, and in particular from his base in Port Royal, Jamaica, that the swashbuckling, moustachioed Henry Morgan acquired his reputation. It should be remembered that, although many of his raids on Spanish settlements in the Caribbean and in

South America were initiated by him, he was licensed to kill by the British government.

Yes, he really was the James Bond of his day, free to attack the Spanish conquerors of the new world at will. Remember, the British had spent rather a lot of time beating each other up in the Civil War, thus allowing the Spanish to dominate the Caribbean. Cromwell and Charles II both recognised the importance to Britain of getting control of the trading routes to America and so supported Morgan and other buccaneers in their activities, even though these privateers made themselves extremely rich with the profits of their activities.

For seventeen years Henry Morgan conducted a series of daring attacks on Spanish settlements and Spanish ships with his crews of buccaneers, before returning to London an extremely wealthy man. Back home he was lauded for his exploits and it was no surprise when in 1685 he was asked to return to Jamaica as acting governor. He was also Vice-Admiral, Commandant of the Port Royal Regiment, Judge of the Admiralty Court and Justice of the Peace. He was a heavy drinker, however, and still preferred the company of those he had sailed with in the rum shops of Port Royal. His drinking probably contributed to his death, which occurred in 1688.

I wonder if the Lesser Horseshoe bats were nesting at St Cadoc's when Henry Morgan was around there in his younger days? Bats are famously sightless but they do have buckin' ears.

Pandy is a tiny settlement on the road between Abergavenny and Hereford, where the influential radical thinker and writer Raymond Williams was born and brought up. Williams has given us a beautiful picture of the idyllic solidarity of a rural Welsh village in the 1930s in his partly autobiographical novel *Border Country*. Here's his description of the fictional Glynmawr, based on the real Pandy:

> *"To the east stood the Holy Mountain, the blue peak with the sudden rockfall on its western scarp. From the mountain to*

> *the north ran a ridge of high ground, and along it the grey Marcher castles. To the west, enclosing the valley, ran the Black Mountains: mile after mile of bracken and whin and heather, of black marsh and green springy turf, of rowan and stunted thorn and myrtle and bog-cotton, roamed by the mountain sheep and the wild ponies."*

The Holy Mountain referred to is The Skirrid, which looks exactly as Williams described it and the rest of the scene I could see as Martin and I came downhill into Pandy itself. The village is situated on the main road from Abergavenny to Hereford at the base of the Black Mountains and within a one-mile stretch of that road there are four pubs, two of which I visited for my research.

The first of these was the Skirrid Inn, which claims to be the oldest pub in Wales and one of the oldest in Britain. There is a record of a court being held here in 1110 when one of the unfortunates in that trial was hanged from the inn beam for sheep stealing, setting something of a morbid precedent. Courts were held within its walls between the 12th and 17th centuries and legend has it that over 180 people were hanged in the Inn from a beam where rope scorch marks can still be seen. It is believed that many of these were sentenced by the notorious "Hanging" Judge Jeffreys who was sent to Wales by the king to brutalise the local population for supporting the Duke of Monmouth in his failed rebellion.

"Hanging" Judge Jeffreys, having had a successful (i.e. brutal) career as Recorder of London under the wonderfully-named Chief Justice Scrogs, became Charles II's Chief Justice, loathed and reviled throughout the land but nowhere more than in Wales. The historian Macaulay described him thus:

> *"(He was) the most consummate bully ever known in his profession...The profession of maledictions and vituperative epithets which composed his vocabulary could hardly have been rivalled in the fishmarket or the beargarden. His yell of fury...sounded like the thunder of judgement day. Even when he was sober, his violence was sufficiently frightful. But*

*in general his reason was overclouded and his evil passions
stimulated by the fumes of his intoxication."*

The Skirrid Inn is an atmospheric place still with its heavy
flagstone floors, ancient stone walls, old wood panelling and its
old ship's bell for calling last orders. Above the ancient fireplace
the landlord used to leave a pot of Devil's Brew - the last of his
ale for the Devil. On the front step he would have left a jug of
Pwcca after his last customer had gone as another appeasement
to the spirits of darkness. Next to one of the bars is the step
on which those about to be hanged were stood and above it
is the beam from which a noose hangs to this day, presumably
no longer in use, even on stag nights. A slate at the bar offers
Hangman's Lunch on its menu.

I would have stayed overnight there but the current owners
have gone for the higher end of the market with their four-poster
beds and I couldn't justify the expense. I merely had a pint of
Usher's Best Bitter and gazed my fill before catching a bus to rejoin
Martin at the Lancaster Arms further down the road. An advert on
the bus for Irn-bru caught my eye, and I swear I am not making
this up. Over a picture of a laughing young blonde woman and
a brylcremed Ronald Reagan lookalike was the speech bubble
emanating from the girl's mouth which proclaimed:

"My two favourite things, Irn-bru and Dick."

What could it possibly mean?

The Lancaster Arms does not claim to have anything like the
atmosphere of the Skirrid Inn but it does cater for walkers. For
a start, one of the beers it serves, produced by the Breconshire
Brewery, is named Ramblers' Ruin and very nice it was too.
Secondly, its menu features a number of walker-oriented dishes,
of which I chose an appetising Ramblers' Ragout. But its best
feature is its landlord, Terry, who positively welcomes walkers
and is an entertainment in himself.

Two other walkers, Roger and Tom from Warrington, who
were coincidentally staying at the same Bed and Breakfast place
as us, joined us at table. They had ordered a starter of garlic
mushrooms and Terry brought it to their table, then noticed that

he hadn't given them cutlery to eat with.

"Sorry about that. I'm a YTS trainee," he explained. "We haven't got to that bit of the course about laying tables yet."

And he went to fetch the necessary.

Tom meanwhile had noticed that there was water dripping on to the bench next to where he was sitting and pointed this out when Terry returned, indicating the bulge in the ceiling plaster where something nasty in the plumbing was clearly occurring.

"Yes, we've had that problem before," stated Terry, hands on hips, gazing at the offending bulge. "But remember I'm only a YTS. Plumbing is next year."

And he promptly placed a towel on the wet bench where the water was dripping through and walked away to serve other customers.

You don't see such nonchalance in the face of dire problems much, nowadays, do you? Everybody's been on these customer care courses nowadays and listened to self-appointed gurus like Ray Kroc, the founder of McDonalds, saying, "The most important ingredient is the customer." Well, not quite, Ray. Personally, I'm all for Terry's studied and laid-back attitude, as long as the beer and the food are good.

Later, having enjoyed my meal, I fancied a final drink, a nightcap to help me sleep, and asked him if he served Irish coffee.

"No," said Terry. "Only instant. Is that any good?"

I wanted to hug the man.

The next day's walk, I have to say, was breathtaking and probably one of the finest day's walking I have ever enjoyed. It began with a steep ascent on to Hatterall Hill but once you've gained the height you then have the pleasure of a ten-mile long ridge walk along the border between England and Wales. I was fortunate that the weather was so good because the peaty ground was quite hard to walk on, which is not the case at damper times of the year, and the views either side of the ridge were glorious. All day I was accompanied by the sweet songs of skylarks, who flew suddenly out of their heather hideouts to pirouette gracefully and tunefully in the sky. It was difficult to believe that this is a threatened species.

A quarter of the way along the ridge, if you're lucky with the weather as I was, you catch your first glimpse of Llanthony Priory downhill to the west. I had originally planned to walk that way but the weather was so splendid on the tops, with a light breeze making the heat and humidity bearable, that I decided to maintain my height. It is believed that St David built the first chapel at Llanthony but the Priory owes its origins to a Norman knight William de Lacy who was so overcome by the peacefulness of the place that he laid down his arms and became a hermit. The Black Canons of the Order of St Augustine, who settled there, were always seen as Norman oppressors by the Welsh, for they brutally oppressed the local population and hanged any miscreants in the abbey's grounds. Gerald of Wales who visited Llanthony in the 12th century, wrote:

"This was formerly a happy, delightful spot, most suited to the life of contemplation, a place from its first founding fruitful and to itself sufficient. Once it was free but it has since been reduced to servitude, through the boundless extravagance of the English, its own reputation for rich living, uncontrolled ambition ... [and] the negligence of its prelates and patrons."

A later visitor who was attracted by the mystery of the place was Alfred Watkins, the inventor of the notion of ley lines. In his famous book *The Old Straight Track*, Watkins revelled in the ancient tracks and hilltop notches that he found around here. According to him, two major ley lines pass through Llanthony. Ley lines he believed were alignments of ancient sites or holy places, such as stone circles, standing stones, cairns, and churches. Nowadays they have been adopted by New Age occultists everywhere as sources of power or energy, attracting not only curious New Agers but also aliens in their UFOs. This ley line business is either a load of baloney, if you're a sceptical old fart like me, or the secret to the universe, if you're that way inclined.

Chances are if you're reading this, you'll tend to the former view. But who knows what is the truth?

Another person to be enchanted with Llanthony was the poet Walter Savage Landor, friend and contemporary of Charles Dickens and Robert Browning. His most famous piece was:

> *I strove with none, for none was worth my strife;*
> *Nature I loved, and next to Nature, Art;*
> *I warmed both hands before the fire of Life;*
> *It sinks, and I am ready to depart.*

It's called *On His Seventy-fifth Birthday* and it couldn't be more untrue about Landor himself, for he was a complete rogue. He was expelled from Rugby School for writing a very rude poem and then expelled from his college at Oxford for firing a gun into the room of a Tory undergraduate (you could forgive him for that, couldn't you?). He then quarrelled with his father and moved to Wales to live. On his father's death he spent his inheritance on raising a private army to go to Spain and fight Napoleon. As neither the British nor the Spanish Governments were interested, he returned to England, sold the family estate and bought Llanthony Priory. Here he planned to start a school, farm merino sheep, and plant ten thousand Cedars of Lebanon.

Four years later, threatened with libel action, he fled abroad and spent the next twenty years wandering through Europe, where he was threatened with expulsion from Florence for libelling the local police. In 1835 he quarrelled with and left his wife and children in Italy to return to England but twenty years later, threatened with another libel action, he fled to Italy again, spending his last years in Robert Browning's villa.

Now does this sound like a man who "strove with none"? I think not. It is curious how the view we have of ourselves rarely meshes with others' perception of us. Ask Neil and Christine Hamilton.

The further I walked along the Hatterall Ridge, with my skylark accompaniment, the closer into view came the Black Hill to the north-east and indeed I met a number of walkers who had reached the ridge by climbing that height. This hill has inspired many over the years and is the subject of Bruce Chatwin's atmospheric novel *On the Black Hill.*

Chatwin is better known as a travel writer but this novel about twin brothers growing up and farming in the area around the Black Hill owes much to the same sort of detailed research that the author conducted for his travel books. In the search for veracity Chatwin interviewed hundreds of local people and built his novel on their shared memories. Here's the twin brothers' father, Amos Jones, waiting in a local pub for a neighbouring farmer with whom he has a dispute:

> *"In the tap-room of the Red Dragon it was a little too hot. Amos sat away from the fire, peering through dirty net curtains on to the street. The barman swabbed down the counter. A pair of horse-dealers in high spirits were swigging at their tankards, and shooting gobs of spit on to the sawdust-covered floor: from another table came the clack of dominoes and the noise of boozy laughter. Outside, the sky was grey and grainy, and it was freezing hard. The clock showed Watkins twenty minutes late. A hard black hat moved up and down the street, in front of the tap-room window."*

The pre-First World War scene is skilfully painted and the rural atmosphere that underpins the narrative of the book, at once never-changing and simultaneously undergoing the transformation that machinery has brought, has an intensely-physical feel to it.

Another artist drawn to this part of the borderlands was Eric Gill, known for his invention of Gill Sans typescript and for large sculptures, such as *The Winds* above St James's underground station in London and panels showing *The Stations of the Cross* in Westminster Cathedral. Gill lived for a time in Capel-y-Ffin on the western side of Hatterall Hill, a few miles north of Llanthony, and tried to build an artistic community there. Gill was another eccentric character whose idiosyncratic Roman Catholicism included a belief in adultery and incest. Recently an archive of materials by Gill has resurfaced after being lost since his brother's death in 1973; it includes beautiful and erotic nude drawings which Gill gave as a gift to his confessor, Monsignor John O'Connor, who was the person on whom G.K. Chesterton based his Father Brown character.

I reached the trig point on Hay Bluff at about one o'clock and paused to take in my final sight of the surrounding countryside from the heights and to have my lunch. Ahead of me were stupendous views over the Wye Valley and further afield to the Malvern Hills in the distance, behind me lay the Black Hill and the Olchon Valley and to my left was the Twmpa, better known as Lord Hereford's Knob. I've naturally never met Lord Hereford and therefore cannot comment on how approximate the design of Twmpa is to his personal equipment, but, if size is anything to go by, he must have had a few problems getting in and out of bed.

From Hay Bluff it was a rapid descent to the Gospel Pass road and then via field paths into Hay-on-Wye which I was surprised to reach by mid-afternoon. I rewarded myself with a couple of pints in the Kilvert Hotel, where I sat in the sunshine and skimmed through the *Daily Mail* that had been left at my table. Among its many titbits was a typically *Mail* diatribe against the European Union Social Affairs Commissioner Anna Diamantopoulou who "wants to hand the courts powers to block TV shows that include stereotypical portrayals of men and women which affront human dignity". Of course, this fed into two of the *Daily Mail's* greatest prejudices - Europe and political correctness. Helpfully, readers were provided with the sort of jokes that would be banned under such proposals, jokes such as:

Q. Why did God invent women?
A. Because sheep can't fetch beer from the fridge.

Q. Why are men like linoleum?
A. Because, if you lay them right, you can walk all over them for the rest of your life.

This was accompanied by a computer-enhanced picture of Ms. Anna Diamantopoulou's head superimposed on that of a bikini-clad model.

Ah, the *Daily Mail*. Where would we be without its frothing at the mouth about the unreal evils of our day?

6 Hay-on-Wye

I suppose with a name like mine I just had to be a bibliophile, didn't I? And being so, it's no surprise that I was drawn many years ago to Hay-on-Wye, the Town of Books, and have been visiting it regularly ever since. Hay is a lovely town, its narrow streets and old market place complemented by fine pubs and, of course, its wonderful array of bookshops. I love wondering around there and never leave without spending large amounts of money on books. Sadly, I wasn't there on 1st April (All Fools Day) 1977 when King Richard, Coeur du Livres, wearing a cardboard crown with cotton-wool around it and bearing an orb made from dipping a ball-cock in gold paint, declared Hay to be an independent kingdom.

As he spoke, the Hay Air Force - a solitary two-seater Beagle plane - circled overhead, dipping its wings every time it passed over the house of the Duchess of Offa's Dyke, while the River Wye was simultaneously patrolled by the Hay navy - a two-man rowing boat. After King Richard had issued his proclamation, an impromptu rendering of the National Anthem for Independent Hay was performed, which bore an uncanny resemblance to *Colonel Bogey*. King Richard then rode through town in his regalia on his horse, which he then renamed Caligula and made Prime Minister. After a spectacular fireworks display (well, a few rockets and suchlike), the town celebrated with a party.

If I had been there, I would have been one of the first to join the Hay aristocracy by buying a fake earldom for £15. You can still, I believe, buy a Hay passport for 75p or a knighthood for a knockdown £2.50. And you can still buy books from King Richard's castle.

So what was going on, you may be asking. And who were

these people?

Well, King Richard is none other than Richard Booth who, as a twenty-three year old bought the old Fire Station in Hay and filled it with second-hand books, bought in huge swathes from libraries or Working Men's Clubs or anywhere. The self-proclaimed Duchess of Offa's Dyke was one April Ashley, formerly merchant seaman George Jameson, whose flamboyant personality and outrageous behaviour drew her to Booth's eccentricities and who settled in Hay as his official consort.

"Old books never die," was Booth's motto and he proved this to be true in spectacular fashion. His business boomed in the early sixties, so much so that within two years he had bought Hay Castle, built originally soon after the Norman Conquest, with the profits from his business. By the mid-seventies he had a staff of twenty and a million books in various bookshops in the town. His success has inevitably led to other booksellers setting up business in Hay, including some who were first trained by Richard Booth. At the last count, this tiny town on the border of England and Wales had thirty-nine bookshops. There used to be regular coach trips from London for bibliophiles seeking rare treasures. Every day sees new visitors who come out of curiosity, or because they think they might find that long-missing Ajax Matchless Handbook circa 1956, or an early edition of some Enid Blyton masterpiece.

The origins of the 'Home Rule for Hay' campaign are hilarious and bear repeating. It began as a joke in the pub where Booth was drinking with friends but somehow, on a slow news day, it became the story that dominated the headlines and then attracted more people to the town. Recent studies have shown the enormous economic benefit to the whole mid-Wales area from the creation of the Town of Books and other towns in Europe and America have copied the idea.

It is a remarkable story and led to the setting up of the annual Hay Literature Festival, which began in 1988 and has been held annually every spring bank holiday week since. It has nothing to do with Richard Booth, who was for many years agin it, although he appears to have mellowed in recent times, even appearing on stage for the first time there in 2002. I just love it. Where else would I get to hear the likes of Toni Morrison, John Mortimer, Van Morrison, Bill Bryson, Jeremy Paxman, Ian McEwan and Melvyn Bragg? All of these I have seen and listened to over the past few years. And at other times the striped marquee has been graced by Maya Angelou, William Golding, Bill Clinton, Margaret Atwood, Eddie Izzard, Courtney Pine and countless other writers and artistes.

I find it just gobsmacking to listen to some of my heroes reading from and talking about their books. Okay, so I may not always agree with their perspectives but the chance to listen is wonderful. I'm afraid I'm a complete groupie at Hay. I hang around waiting to spot authors, as if I was still completing one of those *I Spy* books my parents used to use to keep us kids quiet in the back of the car on long journeys. I once passed within a few feet of Melvyn Bragg and another time stood next to someone who looked remarkably like William Shakespeare in the queue for the Gents. I'm just hopeless, so much so that I suspect you're already getting bored, so I'll stop here.

But, if you've never been to Hay Literature Festival, go. It's a treat, I promise.

If you thought Richard Booth was a bit of an oddball, then you ain't seen nothing yet, for Hay-on-Wye has been home to more than one of these colourful types who make our ordinary lives seem so pale in comparison with the gaudiness of theirs. Take the Reverend Francis Kilvert, if you will, or Francis Pervert, as some would prefer to call him. Kilvert was for seven years between 1865 and 1872 curate to the vicar of Clyro, the tiny village that stands on the opposite side of the River Wye to Hay. For five of those years, for reasons we do not know, he kept a diary, which gives an immaculate record of an agricultural community, still virtually untouched by modern transportation and communication systems. The account he has left us of his time among this community became more widely known when it was first published in 1938 and, in many people's judgement, his diary, written for his own pleasure rather than for publication, has become a minor classic of its period. There is now a thriving Kilvert Society and people flock to Clyro and its surrounding countryside drawn by the notion of visiting Kilvert Country.

So what's the fascination? Let's dip into his writings to find out.

Francis Kilvert was poor but, being a man of the cloth, he had access to rich and poor alike and it is his portraits of some of these that live on in his words. Here, for instance, is one of his favourite parishioners, John Morgan, the old soldier who had fought against Napoleon's armies:

> *Talking of the Peninsular war he said he well remembered being in a reserve line at Vittoria when a soldier sitting close to him on the edge of a bank had his head carried off by a cannon ball which struck him on front on the throat. The head rolled along the ground, and when it ceased rolling John Morgan and the other soldiers saw it moving and 'playing' on the ground with a twitching of the features for five minutes after. They thought it so extraordinary that the subject was often talked over round the camp fire as an unprecedented marvel.*

Here are the less-contented Corfields:

> *Annie Corfield is better but we fear that she and her sisters, the twins Phoebe and Lizzie, are very miserable and badly treated by their father since their mother's death. What would she say if she could see them now, ragged, dirty, thin and half-clad and hungry? How unkindly their father uses them. The neighbours hear the sound of the whip on their naked flesh and the poor girls crying and screaming sadly sometimes when their father comes home late at night.*

But Kilvert can also be rhapsodic in his descriptions of the countryside through which he walks on his visits around the parish:

It was sultry hot climbing the hill though there was the blowing of a wind from the west. In the Chapel field the tall brown and purple grasses were all in billows like the sea, as the wind coursed over the hill driving one billow after another, sheen and dusk, up against the Chapel wall. And the Chapel in the grass looked like a house founded upon a rock in the midst of a billowy sea.

But I suppose you really want to know why some people refer to him as Francis Pervert, don't you? Go on, admit it! There's a bit of a clue in the knowledge that he was at the same Oxford college as Charles Dodgson, a.k.a. Lewis Carroll, the creator of *Alice in Wonderland*, but you really have to look at all Kilvert's diary entries when he comes across very young girls:

Being tub night Polly with great celerity and satisfaction stripped herself naked to her drawers before me and was very anxious to take off her drawers too for my benefit, but her grandmother would not allow her. As it happened the drawers in question were so inadequately constructed that it made uncommonly little difference whether they were off or on, and there was a most interesting view from the rear.

Or what about this gipsy child he finds in the village school?

Since the inspection the classes and standards at the school have been rearranged and Gipsy Lizzie has been put into my reading class. How is the indescribable beauty of that most lovely face to be described - the dark soft curls parting back from the pure white transparent brow, the exquisite little mouth and pearly tiny teeth, the pure straight delicate features, the long dark fringes and white eyelids that droop over and curtain her eyes, when they are cast down or bent upon her book, and seem to rest upon the soft clear cheek, and when the eyes are raised, that clear unfathomable blue depth of wide wonder and enquiry and unsullied and unsuspecting innocence. Oh, child, child, if you did but know your own power. Oh, Gipsy, if you only grow up as good as you are fair.

I think I've showed you enough. And these are merely extracts from the edited diaries. Some of them never saw the light of day, being destroyed by his wife to whom he was married for a mere month before he died of peritonitis in 1879. Did she read stuff that would have condemned him even more?

We'll never know. But, if Kilvert were alive today, the *News of the World* would be frothing in its headlines and inciting his parishioners to march through Hay and Clyro, waving placards that questioned his right to live and demanded at the very least his removal from office immediately and more likely the removal of his genitals. It would be no use him protesting that he was a Victorian gentleman and that there was nothing seen to be odd about his behaviour at the time.

The citizens of Herefordshire would have got your number, Francis. They would remember their sisters in Portsmouth and how they cleaned up their council estate. Wise up! It's time to get out.

And then there was the Poisonous Major.

Herbert Armstrong, five foot six inches and seven stones, starched collar and waxed moustache, took up his post as a solicitor in Hay-on-Wye in 1906. Sixteen years later, on 31st May 1922 in Gloucester Gaol, he achieved the dubious distinction of becoming the only solicitor in the United Kingdom to be hanged for murder. The victim? His own wife, whom he had assiduously courted for many years before their marriage in Hay in 1907.

The story needs some embellishment, I fear, so I will not disappoint you. Armstrong was in many ways a model citizen. After settling in Hay, he joined the local Masonic Lodge, became a churchwarden at one of the churches, set up a company of the Territorial Army and was later appointed Clerk to the Magistrates Court. The advent of war in 1914 was a major setback, however, as his business suffered. When he returned, now a Major from his time in France, he found that a rival solicitor, named Oswald Martin, had set up in town. It appears that he took a dislike for the younger and flashier man, which was to last for some time.

Armstrong had become an overfussy gardener, determined to literally root out even the most stubborn dandelion in his patch and to do so he used to purchase quantities of arsenic from the local chemist, Fred Davies, who just happened to be Oswald Martin's father-in-law. Armstrong's wife Katherine was notoriously tyrannical, telling her husband in company that it was his bath night or that he was drinking too much. Kate, as was the way in those times, supervised the household and played the piano but was well on the way to becoming a top hypochondriac. What began as mild rheumatism developed over a two year period through sleeplessness, mental imbalance, and profound melancholy, into insanity, when she had to be sent away to be minded. Although her mental health recovered enough for her to return home, her physical health did not and her condition deteriorated rapidly until she died.

Armstrong, now lonely, was left to supervise his children's education and to reach a new way of living. Amongst other things, he sought to rebuild his relationship with fellow-solicitor Oswald Martin, inviting him for supper one evening, giving him a buttered scone and a slice of currant loaf. However, the latter on returning home became violently ill and had to be treated by the local doctor for biliousness. Pharmacist Fred Davies, father-in-law of Martin you'll remember, took it upon himself to discuss the illness with the doctor, offering his opinion that his son-in-law had been poisoned. He even produced a box of chocolates, which he claimed had been sent anonymously to the Martins and samples of which they had eaten and subsequently made them ill.

So insistent was Fred Davies that the good doctor decided to take a sample of Oswald Martin's urine and, lo and behold, it contained traces of arsenic. Armstrong was immediately arrested and charged. Meanwhile the doctor obtained an order for the exhumation of Katherine Armstrong's body, which also was found to contain large quantities of arsenic. Writing on the wall time for the poisonous major and, despite the efforts of his defence lawyers, he was found guilty and hanged. His last words, as the hangman adjusted the noose around his neck, were: "I'm coming, Katie!"

The hangman's name was John Ellis, a great Rugby League fan, who met a Rochdale Hornets player in town after the hanging and spent a pleasant hour with him before returning home by train, in time for tea. Ellis was later to be responsible for hanging Dr Crippen and Sir Roger Casement, before he cut his own throat with a barber's razor and died.

Did Armstrong do it? No one knows. If he did, why? Again no one knows. As the judge at his trial said, "To find three and a half grams in a solicitor's pocket is surely rare". And we have to assume his guilt. But Armstrong never told us so it will remain a mystery to alternatively haunt and entertain those of us who come to visit this lovely little town on the border of England and Wales.

Last but not least of Hay's characters has to be Lucy who is the landlady of The Three Tuns pub just before you hit the bridge leaving town. I'd heard a lot about Lucy on previous visits but had never ventured into the pub. From the outside it is not especially attractive, with its pebbledash walls, which apparently hide an ancient timber-framed building.

"Hello, dear," she said as I stepped into the rather dark single room that is The Three Tuns, a room full of personal mementoes, old newspapers, and Lucy sitting on a wooden chair. There were also several birthday cards displayed.

Lucy is an old lady, small and shrivelled but quick-witted and not one to be dealt with discourteously.

"What can I get you?" she continued, still sat in her chair.

I glanced at the bar and saw four barrels sitting there.

"What bitter have you got?" I asked.

'There's the draught or the keg."

"What are the other barrels?" I queried out of curiosity more than anything else.

"Those are cider," Lucy told me. "Local cider."

I knew all about scrumpy and its effects, and quickly decided to stick with the draught beer, which I have to say was deliciously still and hoppy, though I've no idea what brewery it originated from as these barrels contain no markings.

"Who are the birthday cards for?" I asked, for there were only the two of us in the pub.

"It was my birthday on St Lucy's Day. I had a card from Neil Kinnock," she proudly explained.

"Neil Kinnock," I said in surprise. "How d'you know him?"

"He used to come in here before he was a politician. He was a rep. and used to come here to sell me stuff. I can't remember what it was he sold now but I remember switching on the TV one day and seeing him there giving a speech and I was sure I recognised his voice and his face, though he didn't have so much hair by then."

"So how come the card?"

"Some of my friends had heard me talk about him coming here and they traced him through the Internet and told him about my birthday. And he remembered, bless him, and he sent me a card."

She showed me the card, which, as far as I could tell, was genuinely from Kinnock.

"They've all been in here," she went on. "Jules Holland was here during the Festival. Yes, I've known Richard Booth. And April Ashley. They've all been in here."

Lucy is a truly remarkable old lady whose family have the unique distinction of having kept The Three Tuns for seventy-five years. It's a very special place and she is a very special lady, one of Hay's lovely eccentrics.

7 Hay-on-Wye to Kington

For a change, the first part of the next day's walk out of Hay was not uphill. Instead, there is a really pleasant river walk following the River Wye for the first mile or so and then for the next mile you're never that far from views of the river. When you do leave and head into the hills, you see behind you lovely views of the Wye as it wends its looping way towards the sea. The overwhelming impression I have of the morning's walk was the sweet scent of honeysuckle, burgeoning the hedgerows with its golden flowers. It was a scent that would reappear a number of times on the rest of the walk but nowhere was it so pervasive as during this first stage of the morning's walk through forest paths and little-used country roads.

Late morning I was descending a hill named Little Mountain, where the Offa's Dyke Path makes a sudden swing to the right as a farm gate indicates PRIVATE and NO ENTRY. This farm was once the property of the Vaughan family, one of whose members, the Rev. David Vaughan, rector of St Mary's at Newchurch for 33 years, was often visited by Francis Kilvert. On one occasion Kilvert tells of visiting this farm and finding the two young daughters of the family:

> *"...assisting at the castration of the lambs, catching and holding the poor little beasts and standing by whilst the operation was performed, seeming to enjoy the spectacle."*

Earlier that same week he had visited the same children at the village school, where his other interests predominated:

> *"Janet was doing simple division and said she had done five sums, whereupon I kissed her and she was nothing loth.*

> *Moreover I offered to give her a kiss for every sum, at which she laughed.....Shall I confess that I travelled ten miles today for a kiss, to kiss that child's sweet face. Ten miles for a kiss."*

The previous evening I had been watching the television news where a great fuss was being made about the appointment of the Rev. Jeffrey ("Elton") John to the post of Bishop of Reading. The appointment was being opposed by many in the church because Jeffrey John is a shirt-lifter, a pooftah, a queer. That's not what his opponents are saying, of course, but it is what they are thinking. No matter how much they quote from the bible about homosexuality being an abomination in the sight of God and no matter how much they point to a possible schism in the church, what they mean is that they are prejudiced against same sex relationships. Presumably what they would rather have is the kind of secret paedophilia of Francis Pervert or the illicit and denied affairs of priests with women members of their congregations than an openly gay bishop in a long-term relationship with another man. Really! Religious bigotry is probably the worst of the lot, for these people claim to be members of a religion that preaches love towards others as its central tenet.

The irony of the Jeffrey John story breaking as I stomped over the same ground walked by Kilvert some 130 years ago was brought home to me as I paused outside St Mary's church in the sleepy village of Newchurch. There used to be a yew tree in the churchyard, mentioned by Kilvert, which was 1100 years old. Sadly this ancient tree fell in the great storm of 1991; the handrail by the entrance steps and the offertory plate were then made from the fallen tree, as fitting mementoes. The church noticeboard invited dykers and walkers to go inside for refreshments. I duly went into the church and saw the kettle, the water holder, the jar of coffee, the tea bags, the sugar and the appropriate drinking vessels displayed beside a message inviting visitors to help themselves and to contribute accordingly to church funds. I didn't actually avail myself of this lovely, genuinely Christian gesture because I had just had a long cool drink of water but I did appreciate the gesture. Someone had written in the visitors' book, among all the grateful comments, that it was a pity the church was using Nescafé when its makers Nestlé were responsible for the deaths of so many Third World babies and the vicar had responded by replacing the offending item with a Fair Trade jar of coffee.

Big it up for the Rev. T.J. Williams - a true Christian!

An hour and a half later, after another short climb and more sweet-smelling honeysuckle cloying the air, I was sat in the Royal Oak at Gladestry, the first pint of Early Riser bitter already half-glugged while I awaited a cheese and pickle sandwich. Apart from the landlord, there were only three blokes in the bar, two old-timers and one middle-aged fellow. Some years ago in a competition organised, I think, by the BBC, the nation voted Jenny Joseph's *Warning* as its favourite poem. It begins:

When I am an old woman I shall wear purple
With a red hat that doesn't go, and doesn't suit me,
And I shall spend my pension on brandy and summer
  gloves
And satin sandals, and say we've no money for butter.

I was reminded of the sartorial intentions of Jenny Joseph's narrator when I looked at these two old codgers. One wore green sand shoes, his trousers tucked into his socks, and a nondescript baggy sweater; the other wore an old jacket and waistcoat and shapeless cavalry twill trousers, plus brown boots. They had obviously reached that blissful age when they couldn't give a hoot for what others thought of their attire. They had called in to swap chat, have a beer or two and enjoy a cooked lunch. I don't know if it was a daily routine or a weekly one or just a spontaneous getting together, but it seemed to me the sort of thing that is highly to be applauded.

Their conversation was largely about sheepdogs and sheepdog trials, in which the younger man seemed to be a participant. One of the elders produced a small book, which carried details of forthcoming events in the secret world of sheepdog trialling, and his pal perused this with careful attention. I tried to pick out what they were saying but the whole conversation was conducted in a low Herefordshire burr, not helped by the fact that the two elders had probably only about three teeth between them. I struggled to hear but could not so fell back on recalling my favourite shaggy dog story, which goes like this.

A man was driving through the country when his car suddenly stopped. He got out and looked under the bonnet to see if he could find the problem.

"The trouble is in the transmission," a voice behind him said.

The man turned around in surprise, but he only saw a shaggy old sheepdog standing by the road.

"Did you say something?" the man asked.

"I said you'd better check your transmission," the dog replied.

"This is amazing!" the man cried. He forgot about the car and ran to the nearby farmhouse to tell the dog's owner about what had happened.

"Hmmm," said the farmer. "Was it an old grey sheepdog with big, floppy ears?"

"Yes, yes! That's the one!" cried the man.

"Well, don't pay attention to him," said the farmer. "He doesn't know anything about cars."

Just at that moment, the door opened and in walked Tom and Roger, the Warrington Wamblers. They wanted to sit outside to have their lunch so, loth as I was to miss out on the wonders of sheepdog trialling, I agreed to join them.

"Had a brilliant B and B in Hay last night," Tom began, pointing to the sandwiches he'd just unpacked. "Best packed lunch we've had so far."

"Where was this?" I asked.

"The home of the Town Crier, Ken," Roger answered. "Smashing bloke. Told us all about Hay."

"Bet he didn't tell you about The Three Tuns," I said.

"Oh yes, he did," said Tom. "Apparently when he takes people round the town, he always stops there and tells them that this is the oldest pub in Hay."

"And then, very quietly, that this is the oldest landlady in Hay," added Roger.

Just then Martin appeared. I hadn't seen him since I left him at breakfast in Pandy, where he had decided to catch a bus for the next stage of his journey because of blistered feet. I was surprised to find that he had actually walked the Hatterall Ridge the day before and that now, despite the blisters, he was intent on continuing.

As we chatted, one of the old codgers, the green-sandshoed one, emerged from the Royal Oak and climbed into a beat-up old Maestro car. He loosed off the handbrake and let the car roll downhill before engaging the engine with the clutch. It was clearly a well-rehearsed tactic. I don't expect this quiet community needs policing so I'm pretty sure he would never bother with MOT tests or the like. All he needed was a load of scrap metal to get him to the pub and back.

What a blissful existence!

That Thursday afternoon was to be the last of the really hot sunny days on my journey. It was fitting, therefore, that it should take me over the grassy top of Hergest Ridge with glorious views behind me of the Hatterall Ridge that I had crossed the previous day, of the Brecon Beacons rising mistily behind it, and ahead of me the Malvern Hills pushing through the heat haze. The route over Hergest Ridge is another fine walk of about four miles on springy turf through the ferns that wave along the hilltop. Here there is a circular gallop, I guess still used by horse riders, which used to be Kington Racecourse. In the middle of it lies a block of stone known as the Whetstone, to which are attached several legends. During the Black Death in the reign of Edward III, the country folk brought their crops to the stone for the townspeople to collect, and thereby avoid spreading the plague. That sounds quite believable but a better legend claims that the Whet Stone goes down to the water to drink every morning as soon as the cock crows.

Just beyond the racecourse there is a group of monkey-puzzle trees that act as a waymark. The correct Latin name for these trees is Araucaria, which happens also to be the pseudonym of my favourite Guardian crossword-compiler. Araucaria, in real life a retired vicar named John Graham, is known as the Tiger Woods of crossword compiling, an epithet given to him for offering in one of his Saturday specials the clue "Chaste Lord Archer vegetating", an anagram that produces The Old Vicarage, Grantchester - the home of the great Jeffrey and the fragrant Mary.

Walking is one of those activities where you form instant friendships with people you've never met before and will probably never meet again. Once you find that you're walking at a similar pace, that occasionally you stay in the same Bed and Breakfast, or that you meet up in the same pub (and enjoy too much beer there as a consequence), an easy camaraderie forms. The pleasure of this is that the miles can seem less because you're engaged in some kind of desultory conversation but that same conversation can lead you to miss waymarking signs on your route.

I have mixed views about walking alone or with company. When I walked round the canals of the Black Country, my companion was ex-Scaffold member John Gorman and his company was very much a part of the narrative of *Grey Paes and Bacon*, my book about that walk. My walk along the length of the River Severn, recounted in *Dancing with Sabrina*, was done alone, apart from two stretches where I was accompanied by my wife and by a friend. Generally speaking I enjoy walking companionably - good conversation ensues on all manner of things and the talking and walking flow in and out of each other. On the other hand, if the planned walk is to lead to some future publication, it can be irritating to your companion (a) to know that they're likely to feature in that narrative and (b) to have to stand idly by as you visit some monument or building to gather information.

That afternoon on Hergest Ridge caused no such problems. The four of us - Martin, Roger, Tom and I - formed an easy alliance that ambled comfortably over Hergest Ridge and down into the lovely little town of Kington, which announces itself rather cleverly as 'The Centre for Walking'.

You will know that I had consulted the CAMRA guide before

setting off and here my notes led me into some confusion. I had got into my mind that the real ale pub recommended was called The Old Fogey (which I thought was too good a title not to visit), had told the others of this and had arranged to meet at seven o'clock therein to sample its wares. So, after exploring the church of St Mary the Virgin and taken photographs of the Vaughan tomb, I went exploring the town, hoping to identify where The Old Fogey was. Kington is still an independent little town, betraying a healthy individualism that has refused to be swallowed up by national or global commerce, and I particularly enjoyed its small museum. But I could not find The Old Fogey pub anywhere.

Then I bumped into Martin who swore that there was a pub called The Old Tavern that sold real ales but that the place on the High Street with a sign outside stating Wine Vaults was commonly known as The Old Fogey. What were we to do? I chose the Wine Vaults. It is a tiny bar, old-fashioned, a bit musty but just the sort of place that I could imagine CAMRA members choosing. But then I asked what beer was available and discovered that it was Tetley's bitter, masquerading behind an Ansell's badge, which I knew to be false because the Ansell's brewery in the West Midlands closed down years ago. It was too late to change our minds so we had a pint of that rubbish, then went to an excellent little restaurant called The Hungry Fox for our dinner.

I have to say this was one of the finest meals I enjoyed all through my trek. The Hungry Fox had only been open three weeks when we arrived, its proprietor Alan Arm told us, and he was hoping to establish a quality eating place in the town. My experience there that evening suggested he will have no trouble doing so. The Welsh beef steak ("I guarantee it comes from within ten miles of here") was drenched in a delicious cracked pepper sauce, the steamed vegetables had the sort of flavour that only comes from having been recently harvested, and it was all washed down by a couple of excellent pints of Bishop's Finger (a.k.a. Nun's Delight) beer. It somehow seemed appropriate to be drinking Bishop's Finger after my disquisitions on the clergy earlier in the day.

Martin left after the meal but I was still intent on hunting for the real ale pub, so went back through the town to a place I had seen earlier which advertised that it brewed its own beer. It was called the Queen's Head, which I know doesn't sound anything like Old Fogey or Old Tavern or Old Anything, but I was very confused by now.

"Can I have a pint of your own brew?" I asked the barmaid.

"Sorry, it's not on tap yet," she replied with a smile. "They only started making it the other week."

"So why are you advertising yourselves as selling your own brewed beer?" I asked. "I was hoping for some real ale."

"To be honest," she said, lowering her voice conspiratorially, "I wouldn't recommend the home brew. And I work here. If you want real ales, you should go to The Old Tavern. It's out by the roundabout. It's nice in there."

I couldn't be arsed, to tell the truth. I ordered a pint of another local beer and supped it slowly before returning to my lodgings for the night. On the way back I bumped into Tom and Roger. They had found The Old Tavern and had waited there for an hour.

"Smashing place," said Tom.

"Excellent," said Roger. "Pity you missed it."

Sometimes you just have to grin and say nowt.

8 Kington

You wouldn't know it from walking through the sleepy little town of Kington with its 300-year-old black and white houses, its tall clock tower built to commemorate Queen Victoria's 1877 Golden Jubilee and its Norman church, but it is associated with one of the most notable characters in our literature. I'm talking about Conan Doyle's infamous sleuth, Sherlock Holmes, who, complete with deerstalker, magnifying glass, pipe and Dr. Watson, set about solving the mystery of *The Hound of the Baskervilles* in late Victorian times, little knowing that his creator got his inspiration here in Kington.

Now, as any keen Sherlockian (yes, that's what these particular anoraks call themselves) knows, the action in *The Hound of the Baskervilles* takes place on Dartmoor, not on the border between England and Wales. But therein lies, appropriately enough, the mystery. For, you see, Conan Doyle himself said that the idea for the Baskerville hound came from a golfing trip he made to Cromer in Norfolk with a friend. When a storm drove them indoors, the friend entertained Doyle with tales of a phantom dog called Black Shuck, which allegedly haunted the local countryside. Black Shuck was a terrifying creature: as big as a calf, and with eyes that bled fire and anyone unfortunate enough to meet him was sure to die. Conan Doyle and the friend, whose name was Fletcher Robinson, then worked into the night plotting the story. Shortly afterwards the writer went to stay at Robinson's house on the edge of Dartmoor to acquire further material for his story.

So what's all that got to do with Kington?

Well, you see there is a legend in Kington about Thomas "Black" Vaughan of Hergest whose ghost allegedly tormented the inhabitants of the town by taking the form of a fly in order to pester horses and upset farm wagons and then entering the church as a Hereford bull.

Sounds like a load of bull, doesn't it?

Anyway, according to this legend, Black Vaughan so terrified the local peasants that they stopped going to market and the town's prosperity dipped. Now if there's one thing that capitalism can't stand it's making a loss, so Black Vaughan was given the good old bell, book and candle treatment. And that should have been that, except for the fact that Black Vaughan's dog allegedly continued to haunt the territory its master had once operated in. And it is this Black Dog of Hergest which Conan Doyle was told about when he was staying at nearby Clyro Court with one Thomas Baskerville, whose family had lived there for centuries.

Now is that a coincidence or is it a load of cobblers? Make your own mind up.

And here's another neat little twist to this tale. When *The Hound of the Baskervilles* first appeared, it had a footnote on the title page that read:

> *"This story owes its inception to my friend Mr Fletcher Robinson, who has helped me both with the general plot and in the local details. ACD."*

And it is certainly true that Robinson received £30 per 1000 words while Doyle got £100. All the more curious then that Robinson should have died suddenly at the young age of 36, apparently of typhoid. One theory is that he was poisoned by laudanum administered by Doyle, a qualified doctor.

Personally, I know that writers are notorious liars, so I put no credence on what any of them say, even under oath. Conan Doyle may have wanted us to believe that Fletcher Robinson's tale about Black Shuck was the origin of *The Hound of the Baskervilles* but I think he was just protecting his sources.

Trust me, I'm a writer.

In my experience there are two things that get the Welsh stirred up. The first is rugby football, which they play with a passion that sometimes belies their abilities but which has in the past produced those great heroes Gareth Edwards, Barry John, J.P.R. Williams *et cetera*. The second is their brazen insistence that King Arthur and his Knights of the Round Table (and Camelot and Guinevere and Merlin and Excalibur) were Welsh. Now travelling along Offa's Dyke doesn't present you with many opportunities to see Welsh rugby but it does have a real and serious connection to the timeless legends of Arthur.

The Hound of the Baskervilles is not the only literary association present in Kington and once again it is the Vaughans of Hergest who have a hand in this. *The Red Book of Hergest*, so called because of its red leather cover, contains a collection of medieval Welsh manuscripts that many believe to be the most valuable collection in existence. *The Red Book* contains the earliest version of the complete *The Mabinogion* and already I can hear you going "Wow!" with excitement. But, just in case you aren't and you've never heard of *The Mabinogion*, let me enlighten you.

The Mabinogion contains tales from Welsh history and pseudo-history. The best known of these tales are those of Arthur who appears in five of them. This is where the realities of history were converted by the Celtic bards who kept these stories alive over centuries into the rosy-tinted myths that we still pay allegiance to today. Remember how the court of President John F. Kennedy, serial adulterer and love-cheat, was likened to Camelot? Remember the success of that sentimental weepie film with Richard Harris as Arthur? There's even an online fantasy roleplaying game "set in Europe's mythological past, incorporating Arthurian legends, Norse mythology, and Irish Celtic lore".

Wow indeed!

So, I can hear you asking, what has Arthurian legend got to do with Kington? And what has it all got to with the Vaughans of Hergest?

Well, it seems that the Red Book was originally created by three monks working together and was finished some time towards the end of the fourteenth century. It was originally put together for an ancestor of Mary Hopkin called Hopcyn ap Tomas who hailed from the Swansea area. Somehow or other, probably through being nicked during the Wars of the Roses, the book found its way from the descendants of Hopcyn to the Vaughans of Hergest. There it was discovered by scholars during the sixteenth century and it now resides in the Bodleian Library in Oxford.

I'm not going to say any more about the Arthurian legends here because, as you will see later, my journey was to take me deeper into these stories and confront me with further evidence of the continuing presence of Arthur in the Welsh psyche. For now then, be content to know that Richard Harris was nowhere in sight in Kington the night I was there, so I didn't have to listen to him croaking:

> *Don't let it be forgot*
> *That once there was a spot*
> *For one brief, shining moment*
> *That was known as Camelot*

As you come down from Hergest Ridge into Kington itself, you go past the remarkable Hergest Croft Gardens, one of whose claims to fame is that the gardens have been tended by three generations of the same family over 95 years. The Banks family originally came to Kington in the early nineteenth century but it was William Hartland Banks, a keen gardener, traveller and plant collector, who began the Hergest Croft Gardens a century later. He purchased unusual plants and trees being brought into Britain at the time from the Himalayas and Western China by exotically named collectors like Ernest "Chinese" Wilson. His son Richard Alford Banks extended the gardens in the 1950s, adding extensive species of birch and maple, which now form the national collections.

Hergest Croft Gardens are now maintained by the third generation of the Banks family, who have added even more to this wonderful creation. The various areas of the grounds are awash with colour throughout the seasons, whether it be from the spring bulbs or from the strange maples and cedars from the

Himalayan mountains. Then there are the little surprises, such as the magnificent wrought-iron gates purchased from the 1924 British Empire Exhibition, the huge sycamore believed to date from 1800, the extensive and magnificent rhododendrons, and the rare plantings from the Far East beside the China Path.

The whole is just an amazing cornucopia of unusual and colourful plants and trees, carefully laid out to show themselves off in the best possible manner. Whether you're a gardening fan or not, it is nigh on impossible not to be impressed with what the Banks family have done over the past century to create this oasis of beauty in the Welsh Marches.

All this is quite unlike the experience of Thomas Gwyn Jones who purchased an old, run-down, abandoned farm nearby with plans to turn it into a thriving enterprise. The fields were overgrown with weeds, the farmhouse was falling apart, and the fences were broken down. During his first day of work the local vicar stopped by to bless the man's work.

"May you and God work together to make this the farm of your dreams!" he said.

A few months later, the preacher stopped by again to call on the farmer. Lo and behold, it was a completely different place. The farmhouse was completely rebuilt and in excellent condition, there were plenty of cattle and other livestock happily munching on feed in well-fenced pens, and the fields were filled with crops planted in neat rows.

"Amazing!" the vicar said. "Look what God and you have accomplished together!"

"Yes, vicar," replied Thomas Gwyn Jones, "but remember what the farm was like when God was working it alone."

Remember *The Exorcist* - that 1970s movie that got everyone scared silly, that caused teenage girls to wet themselves in the cinema and that led to Mary Whitehouse calling for it to be banned?

No, I never saw it either. But millions of people did and one of the luckiest of those people was the man who composed the music that had been used as its score. The music was called *Tubular*

Bells, its composer was Mike Oldfield and for a time he lived in Kington, moving into a house up by the local golf course bought with the revenue generated by the huge sales of *Tubular Bells*.

There is a story behind all this, of course, and I'm going to tell it to you now.

Mike Oldfield was nineteen when he put together a twenty minute demo tape of multi-tracked guitar made on a cheap tape recorder and hawked the resultant music around various recording studios. It was taken up by Richard Virgin's then new record label and, re-recorded by Oldfield playing a multitude of instruments, became Virgin Records' first major hit record, selling millions of copies and staying popular throughout the nineteen seventies. After it was selected as the theme music for *The Exorcist*, its sales multiplied worldwide.

But that wasn't the end of the story. Oh, no! Oldfield didn't cope too well with the sudden fame and took refuge here in Kington where he built a recording studio in his new house (everyone, but everyone, was doing at the time, weren't they?). And it was there that he composed his second album - the sublimely romantic and stress-relieving (if you're a fan) or the sentimental and boring (if you're a rock critic in need of some angst) *Hergest Ridge*. Now I had walked over the actual Hergest Ridge during the day, half hoping to hear those melodic strains wafting through the green sward to relieve my aching legs as they reached the end of a strenuous day's walking. But, of course, I hadn't.

And you won't hear the sounds of Mike Oldfield's music wafting anywhere around Kington nowadays because he doesn't live here any longer. As befits a multi-millionaire fading rock star, he has a grand pad in Buckinghamshire complete with indoor swimming pool and tennis court and pursues inner peace. He's been doing this all his life, of course, signing up for such things as Exegesis and Tai Chi but he was last heard of placing advertisements for women in Lonely Hearts columns like this:

Very successful, good-looking musician and composer, 43, fun-loving with occasional artistic moods, seeks lovely affectionate lady, 25-35 to share extraordinary life of romance, travel and mutual interests.

Apparently he does this while he's still living with one woman, in order to make sure he has the replacement ready and in place. He claims that he is trying to get rid of the child within himself to allow him to manage a mature relationship.

Personally, I think he's been watching *The Exorcist* too often!

Perhaps the time of Kington's greatest claim to fame was when it was visited by General George S. Patton, the American commander of the Third Army during the Second World War, later responsible for relieving the concentration camp of Buchenwald. Patton's most famous dictum, born of his lifelong love of subtlety was:

> *"We are advancing constantly, and we're not interested in holding onto anything except the enemy. We're going to hold onto him by the nose, and we're going to kick him in the ass."*

This, of course, is a policy more recently adopted by New Labour in its attempts to modernise the National Health Service.

So what was Patton doing in sleepy old Kington?

No, he wasn't preparing to kick the ass of the Welsh nor to walk Offa's Dyke. He was there because Kington Camp was being readied for casualties from D-Day, then about to happen. Kington Camp, in the grounds of Hergest Court, was originally opened as a hospital in 1940 in order to provide a base for troops returning from Dunkirk, that astonishingly brave retreat of the British troops across the English Channel in those little boats captained by Richard Attenborough, Jack Hawkins and Captain Bird's Eye.

By 1944 when the Americans had got involved in the war and were preparing for the D-Day invasion, they too were in need of hospitals for any wounded troops and that is what brought them to Kington Camp, which they expanded greatly. Who knows why Patton visited the camp but there is oral evidence that he did. Other G.I.s spent more time there, many experiencing for the first time the English delights of tea, fish and chips, pubs, and bicycling, while the local Kington girls experienced for the first time the delights of oral sex. I doubt somehow if General Patton enjoyed such simple pleasures, as he prepared to lead his army across the Channel and into France, but, hey! we can dream, can't we?

There's a fascinating account of Kington Camp available from the local museum. It features many personal recollections by British and American soldiers of the days they spent at the camp and it is only from those that you get a real feel for what it must have been like as an ordinary participant in the war. Memories of returning from Dunkirk with no weapons, of soldiers with shattered nerves seeking billets, of makeshift concert parties and dances in the deprived conditions. And later memories of film shows at the camp, of twelve-hour passes, of entanglements with the local Kington police, and then of souvenir hunting in Germany.

It's curious that this sleepy little backwater of Herefordshire should have connections with such monumental events as the Dunkirk retreat and the D-Day landings but, as General Patton himself once said:

I don't measure a man's success by how high he climbs but how high he bounces when he hits bottom.

Eat your heart out, George W! You'll never equal those for words of wisdom.

9 Kington to Knighton

The stretch of the Offa's Dyke Path between Kington and Knighton that I walked that Friday is considered by many walkers to be the finest part of the whole walk, largely because it actually is on top of the extant dyke for a large part of the journey. Just over a mile after leaving Kington, you're actually walking along the first section that you've seen for the best part of 55 miles. And it is a terrific feeling to suddenly find yourself, some time after crossing the highest golf course in England, up on Rushock Hill, exposed to the elements but striding along Offa's Dyke itself. Sadly, exposed to the elements meant exactly that as a shower of rain began to fall, displacing the hot weather I had been enjoying for the four previous days.

The previous sections of the Dyke that I had walked, at Sedbury and at Redbrook, were both in wooded areas and it is only when you are on it in the sort of open ground on Rushock Hill that you realise how much of a barrier it must have looked to the Welsh hill farmers. The Dyke continues around Herrock Hill but the Path follows a well-worn track through the ferns and downhill and then, after a short road stretch, along a track past an old farmhouse known as Burfa House. According to the Royal Commission on the Ancient and Historical Monuments of Wales, or RCAHM to give it its snazzier title, this is what is known as a vernacular house built in three main phases and is one of only a few remaining in the country. The first phase of building saw a downhill-sited cruck-framed hall-house erected in1487. In 1502 a close-studded, jettied, storeyed solar wing replaced the upper end bay, and a cross-gable was inserted over the upper end of the hall. Then in 1643 the stair projection was added and the hall enlarged with ovolo-moulded timber detail. Wall paintings survive on the hall side of the solar and within the wing.

Vernacular-house anoraks will know exactly what this all means. I haven't a clue.

On the top of the hill above Burfa House is an Iron Age hillfort known as Burfa Camp, though it was a more permanent base than that name suggests. In the thousand years before the birth of Christ there was a marked change in the way people lived in Britain, as people began to fortify their villages, often situated on hilltops for greater safety. Excavation has shown that some hillforts had a shrine or temple, often near the centre, while others had storage or rubbish pits. Many hillforts cover a large area and would probably have had open ground where domestic animals would have been sheltered in times of trouble. As well as farmers the hillforts were home to craftsmen, bards and warriors whose sport it was to rustle their neighbours' cattle.

And then, as you come out of the forested path that guards Burfa Camp, you're back on the Dyke itself again. This stretch includes an obvious gateway in the Dyke, a sort of Checkpoint Charlie of its day perhaps, controlling entry and exit, though we don't really know if that was what went on. Were there border guards pointing their bows and arrows and shouting out "Achtung!" at any encroaching Taffies? Did the Welsh sheep drovers need passports to herd their fleecy charges through these gaps in the Dyke? Not very likely, given that the Mercians were illiterate, but I suppose some basic form of identification may have been used. Who knows?

Just to the west of Checkpoint Charlie is the wonderfully named village of Evenjobb. This conjured up thoughts in me of the villain's villainous assistant in the James Bond movie *Goldfinger* - remember Oddjob, with his skimming bowler hat that could cut you in half if you didn't get out of the way quick enough? Oddjob, played by actor Harold Takata in the film, has to be one of the most famous henchmen in film history. As with most henchmen, his job was to do the all the killing while Goldfinger went about his normal business. When Goldfinger lost a game of golf, Oddjob demonstrated the world famous steel-rimmed bowler hat, throwing it at a stone statue and cutting its head off.

He seemed to be Goldfinger's chauffeur, bodyguard, caddy and anything you care to mention. Oddjob was the hard knock, but in the end James Bond got the better of him by grabbing Oddjob's hat and throwing it at some steel bars. As Oddjob reached for it Bond touched the bars with a cut electric cable, electrifying Oddjob in an impressive death scene.

Apparently, however, Evenjobb's origin is less dramatic than that. I am told it means Even's copse or wood and was formed as a parish in 1870, when it was given the Welsh name of Evencoed after the nearby Evencoed Court manor house. Another explanation is that in 1267 it was called Emynghop, meaning Emma's valley, but that is disputed and who the hell was Emma? None of this explains the unusual second part of the word - 'jobb'. Since when did this mean 'copse' or 'valley'? I prefer to think that my James Bond fantasies may be closer to the mark and that the village was founded by Oddjob's more saintly brother.

Two miles to the east of the Path lies the town of Presteigne, once the county town of the once-county of Radnor. I had half thought to detour there for lunch and a visit but by this stage it was raining rather steadily and I didn't really fancy adding a further four miles to my journey, especially since I had planned to finish the first stage of my journey in Knighton that afternoon and had a train to catch.

Presteigne is another attractive border town, with its classic Broad Street housing the Judge's Lodging. The town is somewhat unexpectedly on the English side of Offa's Dyke simply because the Mercians captured it, though the Welsh tried to recapture it on a number of occasions, notably under Llewellyn in the thirteenth century and under Owen Glendower in the fifteenth. Its position on the main coaching routes joining London to Cheltenham and Gloucester and eventually to Aberystwyth made it the obvious place for the County Assizes to be held and it is the story of the latter that is beautifully illustrated in the Judge's Lodging housed in the old Shire Hall. Here you can take a trip through the history of the court system, guided by audiotapes that seek to replicate the voices of some of the actors in that system. So, for instance, in the reconstructed courtroom you can hear the trial of William "Quack Quack" Morgan, the local duck thief, while looking out for the open flame gasolier and the vents that blew heat from the gasolier up the judge's trousers to keep his genitals warm. Or you can listen to the booming voice of actor Robert Hardy in his role as local worthy Richard Lister Venables, Chairman of the Magistrates Bench and also coincidentally the man who employed Kilvert.

You will particularly enjoy finding out about life downstairs in the Servants' Hall, where the local dignitaries introduced open-flame gaslights in order to test them out on the servants for safety. No such thing in the Dining Room, of course, where the Judges would have their evening meals. In this very masculine room with its heavy red drapes and huge, dark portraits of other local worthies, the lighting was by beeswax candles only, since it was believed that gas and oil lamps would taint the food. Nowadays we test new things on the populations of Third World countries before we try them ourselves. It's called globalisation.

> *... there came*
> *A post from Wales loaden with heavy news;*
> *Whose worst was, that the mighty noble Mortimer*
> *Leading the men of Herefordshire to fight*
> *Against the irregular and wild Glendower,*
> *Was by the rude hands of that Welshman taken,*
> *A thousand of his people butchered;*
> *Upon whose dead corpses there was such misuse,*
> *Such beastly, shameless transformation,*
> *By those Welshwomen done, as may not be*
> *Without much shame re-told or spoken.*

What exactly did these Welshwomen do? Let's backtrack a moment first. This is Shakespeare's version, told so graphically in the opening scene of King Henry IV (Part 1), of the Battle of Pilleth, which took place by the River Lugg just over a mile to the west of the Offa's Dyke Path. We'll find more about Glendower much later in this narrative but he was a serious problem to Henry and the real Battle of Pilleth in 1402 was a major setback to the Anglo-Norman monarchy. Glendower had led an army into Radnorshire and been met with a force of Herefordshire's finest squaddies, led by Edmund Mortimer.

The Mortimers are inextricably tied up with the Marches. In fact, they were known as the Lords of the March. The dynasty began in England with Ralph de Mortimer, being given lands by William the Conqueror in Shropshire and Herefordshire. From then on for the next few centuries there were regular ding-dongs between the Mortimers and the Welsh until another Ralph married Gwladus Ddu verch Llywelyn Fawr "the Dark Eyed" (Gladys to you and me), daughter of Prince Llywelyn Fawr ap Iorwerth "The Great", in 1230. Our dear Queen Brenda can claim descent from this marriage, so you know it must have involved some trading of highly intelligent genetic material, eh?

There were several more Rogers and Edmunds until yet another Edmund married Philippa, Edward III's granddaughter, who produced a sprog also called Edmund or was it Roger? Anyway one of these was actually the heir to the throne but never got there, so Edmund Mortimer was a bit miffed with Henry IV (Parts 1 and 2) and so was probably only half-hearted in his approach to Pilleth.

Now whether the Herefordshire squaddies had been drinking too much scrumpy or what I do not know, but they took a terrible thrashing, largely because Mortimer's archers turned their bows on their own colleagues and the subsequent slaughter was horrific. Up to 1100 out of a force of maybe 2000 were killed and the defeat sent shock waves though the English court. Mortimer himself was captured and, when there was no immediate ransom for his return from Henry IV, he threw in his lot with Glendower and married the latter's daughter. Since Mortimer's claim to the throne was arguably better than that of Henry IV, this was a cause of serious worry.

There is a tradition in the area that the bodies were buried in a mass grave on the hillside above the church in Pilleth and six

Wellingtonia trees were planted to mark the site. The trees are certainly still there, though there is no official record of their planting.

But, as for the Welshwomen, what were they doing? Thomas Walsingham, the history-writing monk from St Albans, says that the dead bodies were "obscenely mutilated" and I take it to mean that there was a large amount of chopping off of peckers. I imagine they were used for the Welsh equivalent of cockaleekie soup.

By mid-day I had been rejoined by Martin, Tom and Roger and we walked pretty much together along further impressive stretches of the actual Dyke through the steady rainfall. I guess we had all hoped that the rain would let up enough for us to stop and have some lunch but it didn't. Luckily, about two miles from Knighton we found a wooden bus shelter, with a handily placed litterbin, and took some refuge. Tom and Roger were continuing the following day, intent on completing the whole walk by the following Thursday, while Martin was postponing his trek on the northern part of the Offa's Dyke Path to next year. As I've already indicated, I was finishing that day in order to go home for a couple of days rest with the intention of resuming the following Monday.

So, suitably refreshed, we ventured out into the rain again and soon found ourselves coming off the Knighton golf course and down through Frydd Wood and out on to the road above Knighton with the unusual name Under Frydd Wood. I had passed the sign for this road many times, always to be reminded of that classic Dylan Thomas play for voices *Under Milk Wood*. Did Thomas ever come this way and see that road sign? I doubt it. I think it is just a coincidence. Nevertheless the sight of it that wet afternoon, as on every other occasion I have driven or walked past it, was enough to trigger the lines that open Thomas's magnificent word picture:

To begin at the beginning. It is spring, moonless night in the small town, starless and bible-black, the cobble streets silent and the hunched, courters'-and-rabbits' wood limping invisible down to the sloeblack, slow, black, crowblack, fishingboat-bobbing sea.

And I found myself thinking of Rosie Probert and Nogood Boyo and the Reverend Eli Jenkins and Mrs Ogmore-Pritchard and Willy Nilly and Polly Garter and blind Captain Cat and that whole cast of wonderfully-eccentric characters that teem on to the stage in Thomas's words.

And so into the car park behind the Knighton Hotel. It was still only just two o'clock in the afternoon, so I suggested a drink in the Horse and Jockey and we entered a bar which was tastefully decorated in purple concentric circles, presumably to entice the artistic members of the alcopop-swilling youth, where we ordered pints of Speckled Hen and toasted a successful walk so far. There had been a power cut, so there was only candlelight in the bar but I, in my usual post-walking confusion, forgot that this also applied to the toilets where I went to change out of my wet gear into something drier. That's why I was standing in my underpants on the cold floor when some guy came in for a pee.

"Stardate twenty seven zero six zero three. Just popped down to earth for a piss. Natives surprised to see me. Strange dress," he said with a grin, holding an imaginary transporter to his mouth.

"Sorry, I was just…" I tried, pointing at the urinals.

"Natives making strange gestures, Could be trouble. Beam me up, Scottie."

I don't know who was more embarrassed.

After another pint and farewells to my walking compatriots, I left the Horse and Jockey to head off in the direction of the railway station. My train was due to arrive just after four o'clock. By half past four it still hadn't arrived and, since the station was unstaffed, I phoned a number on one of the posters and was told that the train was thirty minutes late because of an electricity failure in the area. Trains, you see, do not run on candlepower.

When it eventually arrived, I clambered aboard and found a seat.

"You've got a return ticket, I suppose," the conductor said glumly.

"No, I just want a single to Shrewsbury," I replied. "I've been walking Offa's Dyke."

I was still in a state of euphoria for completing the first part of the walk with no blisters and no other physical problems, so different from my previous expeditions. The conductor, however, was not impressed. He played with some digits on his machine.

"It's cheaper if you have a return ticket," he said eventually. "Five pounds seventy."

"I don't want a return," I answered. "I just want a single."

"But it's cheaper, you see," he insisted. "Special offer."

"Can I use the return on Sunday?" I asked, suddenly clicking that I would be returning to Knighton in two days time.

"No, it's just a day return."

"So is there another train tonight?"

"No, this is the last one."

"And you mean to tell me it's cheaper for me to buy a day return when I can only travel one way with it than to buy a single ticket?"

"Yes, I'm afraid so. It's a special offer. Look."

He showed me the print out on his ticket machine. Sure enough the day return was thirty pence cheaper than the single ticket. I shook my head and bought it.

"What a way to run the railways," I said.

He shrugged and moved off.

Special Offa, indeed.

10 Knighton

Arriving dry and thirsty at Knighton, or Tref-y-Clawdd (the Town on the Dyke) as it should more appropriately be known, you are spoiled for choice. There's a veritable array of good pubs, there's Ginger's Café, now rebranded as JD's, where you can purchase "real" chips and where allegedly you can hear stunning swearing that outdoes Royston Vasey, or there's Harry Tuffin's supermarket for a wide range of well-priced alcoholic and non-alcoholic drinks. I must admit to having a bit of a thing about Harry Tuffin's - I used it as the place where my fictional Detective Chief Inspector Tallyforth, bought a bottle of Jacob's Creek to accompany him on his bird-watching at the start of his first adventure in *The Llareggub Experience*. I guess it's the name that attracts me. Harry Tuffin - so much more romantic sounding than Tesco or Sainsbury or Safeway. Tref-y-Clawdd was the conclusion of the first half of my journey on Offa's Dyke and the starting point for the second half.

Knighton is also the home of the wonderful Offa's Dyke Centre at the far end of the town, where you are greeted by King Offa himself, or rather a slightly dodgy-looking model of him sat on a stool in the front window. He looks rather worried, as if he's not sure about calling something Offa's Dyke in case it might cause later generations to wonder about his sexual leanings. However, once inside the centre you are assailed by treats galore. There are interactive displays which give you fascinating insights into the construction of the Dyke, the Welsh Princes of the Anglo-Saxon period, the flora and fauna of the area, environmental considerations, the history of Knighton and the activities required to maintain the Dyke and the Long Distance Footpath. It's all done beautifully in a spacious and well-lit room and you can while away a very pleasant hour or so there. And it is absolutely free!

The centre is also the administrative headquarters of the Offa's Dyke Association, who oversee the maintenance of the footpath and its waymarking, and of the Tourist Information Centre, where I discovered a number of other interesting facts about Knighton and its surrounding district.

Did you know, for instance, that the Wales Tourist Board are promoting Wales as the Celtic Hollywood? Listen to this from their advertising bumf:

Directors and producers spend millions trying to capture scenes of beauty, of the wilderness, of lands that are the very source of myth and legend, lands that caress the mind and turn the heart with romance. Here, in Cymru, are ten thousand square miles of scenery, the finest locations that you could wish for, perhaps the best film locations in the whole of Europe. It is not surprising that so often the adventurous director has found his or her way to the land of Wales in search of such scenery. From the 1930's onwards the country has been a source of inspiration to producers, attracting famous international stars including Anthony Hopkins, Gregory Peck, Sophia Loren, Richard Gere, Julia Ormond, Sean Connery, Ingrid Bergman, Omar Sharif, Meg Ryan, the list runs into hundreds.

Now you can't help but be impressed with that, can you? If I were Stephen Spielberg, I'd be hotfooting it to Wales tomorrow. Why bother with the sunny sierras of Spain, the ancient hilltowns of Tuscany or the fleshpots of Florida? Wales sounds the wannabe film set to beat all film sets. And then I read that the first film in their list of famous films produced in Wales is none other than that remarkable, prize-winning, heart-stopping, tear-jerking movie that entranced millions around the globe - *Carry on up the Khyber!* What could be more persuasive than that?

Knighton itself has featured as the location for a couple of filmed ventures. There was *Second Best*, a film that starred William Hurt as loner Graham Holt, who suddenly wants to become a father, leading to his adopting a moody ten-year-old, whose mother has died and whose father is in prison. Before the adoption is complete, the two are allowed to live together, although James is unwilling to accept Graham as his father, maintaining hope that he will be reunited with his real dad. When Graham is finally given permission to adopt the boy, his dad re-appears - stricken with AIDS. That sounds like a lot of fun, eh? Not surprising that it didn't ever get released in the United Kingdom.

Then there was the BBC series *Mortimer's Law*, that starred Amanda Root as Rachel, a strong-headed London barrister who has given up a lucrative career to become a coroner in rural Wales. Of course, as is the way in such series, the number of murders, poisonings, suicides and other violent accidents increases dramatically after her arrival and by the end of the series you wondered how many people were still alive in Knighton, whose grey slate roofs and ancient buildings feature clearly in the programme's opening sequence.

But you'll be pleased to know that *Carry on up the Khyber* was not filmed anywhere near here, though I understand that there is a Sid James lookalike to be found regularly in Ginger's Café.

A couple of miles out of Tref-y-Clawdd lies Stanage Park, where another BBC series was filmed - *Blott on the Landscape*, from the novel of the same name by that comic genius Tom Sharpe. Stanage Hall became in this wonderful retelling the fictional Handyman Hall, ancestral home of the monumentally unattractive Maud Handyman (Geraldine James) who is wooed and wed by Sir Giles Lynchwood (George Cole) who had made his fortune by recognising "potential advantage in unprepossessing properties". Due to a pre-marital agreement, the only way he can get some money for Handyman Hall is by arranging to have a new motorway put through and Handyman Hall made the subject of a compulsory purchase order. But Giles could not take into account the actions and problems caused by the numerically obsessed Ministry of Environment troubleshooter Dundridge (Simon Cadell) or Lady

93

Maud's adoring gardener Blott (David Suchet). The whole thing is a monumental hoot from start to finish, capturing perfectly the black humour that is Sharpe's characteristic style.

Stanage Park was originally laid out by that great landscape gardener, Humphrey Repton, the man who actually invented the term "landscape garden". Repton continued and developed the work of his predecessor as Britain's premier garden designer, Capability Brown, but was most famous for introducing a new element to such work. Because he was anxious for his employers to see what he proposed to do, he devised an ingenious book with a system of sliding panels. Each plate shows a park or garden in its original condition before Repton's proposed improvements; an overlay lifts or slides back to reveal the proposed alterations. In the text, Repton discusses the relationship between landscape gardening and architecture in chapters on colour, interiors, prospects, water, fences and other subjects. These came to be known as Red Books and it is one of these, still extant, that indicates Repton's original design for Stanage Park.

I'm not sure old Humphrey wouldn't have turned in his grave if he'd found out that Stanage Park was actually used as a base for American and Canadian troops during World War Two. Maybe Sir Giles would have found some way of selling them some dodgy black market sausages. Or maybe the scheming Blott would have found ways of keeping the Yanks off his flower borders and relieving the soldiers of their cigarettes at the same time. What is certain is that their presence gave a bit of a boost to the local economy and to the sex lives of the local girls, whose boyfriends had been sent off to Europe to fight the Hun.

There is another fascinating event that may be associated with Stanage. It is claimed that the Early Medieval motte and bailey mound at Stanage Farm is actually the site of Vortigern's burial. Now Vortigern, in case you'd forgotten, was the British king who got the blame for inviting the Angles and Saxons to sail from Germany and settle in our green and pleasant land. Legend has it that he sent a party invitation to Hengist and Horsa, explaining that it was good time for beating up the Picts, but, when they saw all the hops growing in Kent, they decided that they could open their own brewery so they beat up Vortigern as well and took over the land. This all happened somewhere around 450 A.D. near Salisbury when, according to the ever-reliable (ha ha!) Geoffrey of Monmouth, the Brits and the Saxons were at a peace conference and Hengist gave the order *"Nimet our saxes"* which means something like "Okay, boys, show 'em your sex machines". And they did. And that's why the Britons are in Wales to this day and the Saxons, Angles and Jutes took over England.

The anonymous *Stanzas of the Graves* tell that Vortigern, who was also allegedly the forefather of the legendary Arthur, was buried at a place known as Ystyuacheu. By some clever scholarship with Welsh place names, which I won't bore you with here, experts conclude that this unlocated place might well be Stanage.

Well, it's good enough for me. Vortigern's grave - a real blot on the landscape!

Remember:

"The ladies of the harem of the court of King Caractacus were just passing by"?

Altogether now:

"The fascinating witches who put the scintillating stitches in the britches of the boys who put the powder on the noses of the faces of the ladies of the harem of the court of King Caractacus , were just passing by".

How could you forget that dire Rolf Harris number that somehow entered the nation's consciousness way back in the mid-1960s? Well, you didn't, did you? And, now that I've reminded you, it will be running round in your head and driving you absolutely stark raving bonkers for the next two to three hours.

So why am I doing this to you? Well, simply to get you to appreciate that one of the possible sites of Caractacus's last stand is here just outside Knighton. It's a hillside that is actually called Caer Caradoc and it's one of several that lay claim to being where the British king Caractacus fought his final battle against the invading Roman army in 51 A.D. and lost. I'm not going to go into the whys and wherefores about this or any of the other sites but I'm quite happy to accept that this was the actual site of the battle, if only because it's on my route!

Now we know about Caractacus, or Caradoc, because his story was recorded by the Roman historian Tacitus, who tells us how Caractacus, one of the rulers of Britain when the Roman army began its conquest in 43 A.D., retreated before the oncoming legions until he decided to fight one last fight. The superior armoury of the Romans defeated him and he was captured and sent as a prisoner to Rome, where Tacitus takes up the story:

> …*his body was mostly naked and painted with figures of beasts; he wore a chain of iron about his neck, and another about his middle; the hair on his head hanging down in curled locks covered his back and shoulders. Caradoc neither by his looks nor language pleaded for mercy, and when he came before the Emperor's seat expressed himself in these terms:- "Had I made that prudent use of my prosperity, which my rank and fortune would have enabled me to make, I had come hither rather as a friend than as a prisoner; nor would you have disdained the alliance of one descended from illustrious ancestors, and sovereign over many nations. My present condition, disgraceful as it is to myself, reflects glory on you. Possessed as I once was of horses, men, arms and wealth, what wonder is it if I parted from them with reluctance. Had I sooner been betrayed, I had neither been distinguished by misfortune nor you by glory. But if you now save my life I shall be an eternal monument of your clemency." The Emperor generously granted the pardon of Caradoc, his wife and brothers, who remained at Rome in the highest esteem.*

Now what puzzles me about this is that presumably Caractacus would have been speaking British (or Welsh, as we would call it nowadays), while the emperor and all the hangers-on would only have understood Latin. So how did they know what the Ancient Brit was saying? I smell a rat somewhere.

So there you are, Osama Bin Laden. If you want George Dubya Bush to pardon you, you'd better start practising your speech in Arabic now. Who knows? Dubya might just have woken up and think you were saying nice things to him.

On 19th August 1858 a monumental event occurred at Knighton. Accompanied by a salute of cannons, a peal of bells from the church, and two bands, the good citizens of the town marched down to the site of the new railway station, where a grand opening ceremony was enacted. The railway had arrived, bringing with it coal from South Wales, fish from the Pembrokeshire ports, heavy goods from the Black Country, and sheep from the Radnorshire hills. It would take local farmers and their families to market and holidaymakers on trips to the seaside. It would, in time, bring city dwellers to sample the country air and later wounded soldiers back from the battlefields of World War One and later still their American and Canadian counterparts of World War Two to be billeted at Stanage Park.

The railway made a huge difference to Tref-y-Clawdd, bringing goods and passengers and providing a conduit for outgoing goods and passengers. It encouraged a rash of new building projects, including the Central Wales Hotel, which is now rebadged as The Kinsley, together with depots for timber, animal feed, fertiliser, seed, and so forth. An amusing sideline to this development was a building known as The Round House, built in 1880 just across the national border in England and intended as a hotel. Now, as the drinkers among my readers will know, it used to be impossible to slake your thirst on a Sunday in much of Wales until recent years. I can remember having to make do with large quantities of milk when once holidaying in Tenby as a twenty-something laddo. The Round House would have been a brilliant opportunity for Knighton's drinkers to bypass the chapel lawyers, but the latter made such a fuss that the hotel never opened as such, becoming a lodging house for railway workers instead.

The Central Wales Railway that eventually emerged from the rampant privateering that created our railway system covers 120 beautiful miles through the heart of Wales, stretching from Shrewsbury to Swansea. Although it no longer carries freight and Knighton station is now unstaffed, the line somehow survived the savagery of Dr Beeching and his 1960s cuts and provides a crucial lifeline still to the mid-Wales towns. Just listen to the music of the place-names it goes through - Church Stretton, Craven Arms, Broome, Hopton Heath, Bucknell, Knighton, Knucklas, Llangunllo, Llanbister Road, Dolau, Penybont, Llandrindod Wells, Builth Road, Cilmeri, Garth, Llangammarch Wells, Sugar Loaf Mountain, Cynghordy, Llanwrtyd Wells, Llandovery, Llanwrda, Llangadog, Llandeilo, Ffairfach, Ammanford, Pontardulais, Llangennech, Bynea, Llanelli, Gowerton.

Can you be unmoved?

Do you know what a NEO is? Do you even care?

Well, you should, because a NEO is a Near Earth Object, in other words an asteroid or comet, and there's a place a couple of miles south of Knighton which is keeping watch for these NEOs in order to warn the world about their threat to peace and stability. Impressive, eh? And you probably didn't even know the Spaceguard Centre existed nor that it is the hub of the Comet and Asteroid Information Network (yes, that's right, CAIN is its rather worrying acronym).

So, where do NEOs come from? Why do they collide with earth? How often do impacts occur? What would happen if an impact occurred? Could we stop an impact? Should we be worried?

Well, you'll find the answer to some of these questions at the Spaceguard Centre, which used to be known as the Powys County Observatory, although it was built and owned privately as it still is. The current overseer of the Spaceguard Centre is one Jay Tate, an ex-army officer, who gives a fascinating tour of the night skies in his observatory, prior to leading you towards his explanation of NEOs and what a potential danger they are to the human race.

Now it would be easy to laugh at all this if you are, like me, sceptical about people who claim to have seen spaceships or who believe that crop circles were created by little green men from Mars rather than ruddy-faced farmers on tractors. But then why is NASA taking all this so seriously that it has a permanent virtual exhibition about NEOs on its website? And why do some scientists (yes, those guys in white coats and spectacles) talk about the many ways in which the orbit of even a billion tonne NEO could be changed so that it missed the Earth, including attaching solar sails or engines to the object and the use of chemical or nuclear explosives? And why is the British government supporting research into NEOs?

OK, here's the theories. American scientists claim to have evidence that a massive asteroid struck the Earth two hundred and fifty millions years ago, wiping out many early forms of life. A smaller asteroid strike, they say, was responsible for the extinction of dinosaurs more than sixty million years ago. Just over two million years ago, according to some British scientists, an asteroid struck the Southern Ocean, south west of Chile. If the collision had occurred a few hours earlier, southern Africa might have been wiped out, along with our ancestors.

.A few hours! That kind of puts things into perspective, doesn't it? Imagine, if that asteroid had wiped out early humankind, you wouldn't be able to be prompted by my lucid prose to drive to the Spaceguard Centre at Knighton to gaze through its huge telescopes into space or to pick out the planets and stars portrayed in the Planetarium.

Just think what all those of our forefathers who came through Tref-y-Clawdd would have done if they had had access to those telescopes. Would Caractacus have been able to escape from the Roman army? Would Henry IV's soldiers have won the battle of Pilleth? Would Offa have been able to see the full length of his dyke? Would Ginger's Café still stand?

It fair makes you think, eh?

11 Knighton to Montgomery

There's not a lot to do in Knighton on a Sunday afternoon. The prevailing sound, when I arrived there late on to find my Bed and Breakfast prior to resuming my trek, was of drum n' bass being pumped out of pubs and beat-up old Ford Escorts roaring up and down the High Street. It was hot and sticky and unsurprisingly thunder was forecast. That evening I met a couple of the local citizens.

First of all there was the old cap in The Plough who, when I told him I had links with Wolverhampton, informed me that he'd once had a trial for the Wolves when he was fifteen in 1957, but then he'd discovered beer. He was exactly the same age as me but looked fifteen years older. As I walked through the cemetery a little later, I reflected on the number of sixty year olds that were buried there. Or was I just being over-sensitive?

Then there was the landlord of the George and Dragon where I went for my evening meal who told me of the Knighton Town Criers Competition.

"They come from all over," he told me. "Not just from Wales. From all over."

"Friends of mine stayed with the Town Crier in Hay last week," I said, thinking of Roger and Tom's account of their host at the Bed and Breakfast. "Big bloke, apparently."

"Oh yes, some of them are huge," he said. "But not all of them."

"What do they do?" I asked. "Do they see who can shout 'Oyez, oyez, oyez' the loudest?"

"No, there's all sorts of things," he said. "Here you are, here's a leaflet about it."

The leaflet didn't tell me much other than the date of the event, which was mid-August but the British championship of the Loyal Company of Town Criers, held earlier this year in Halifax, gave awards for the best cry, best content, best escort's costume and best couple's costume. The Town Criers were required to deliver their "home cry" which tells the audience about the crier's home town or district and then to give a cry about a notorious character. Sounds like fun, eh?

I have to say that, fascinated as I was in all this, I did not enter the date in my diary.

The Official guidebook warns you that the climb up Panpunton Hill just outside Knighton is a bit of a wake-up call and a preparation for the toughest stretch of the entire Offa's Dyke Path. Because the hills are actually going east to west here, the Dyke is constantly going up and down hillsides, which gives it the feel of a switchback. Very quickly at the bottom of Panpunton Hill I was on the Dyke itself and, even in the rain and cloud that I was experiencing that Monday morning, it is a remarkable structure for a large part of this day's walk. What struck me most where the Dyke marches over the top of Panpunton Hill was how it has become the home for hundreds of cotton-tailed bunnies, who scurried in and out of their burrows as I approached. Odd to think that it is not Saxon warriors guarding the borderlands nowadays but Bright Eyes, Peter, Brer, Flopsy and their kin.

Even in the mist on top I could make out the impressive thirteen-arch Knucklas railway viaduct crossing the River Teme in the distant valley. Further on the green line of the dyke goes over Llanfair Hill. Lord John Hunt, the leader of the successful 1953 Everest expedition, lived in Llanfair Waterdine at the bottom of the hill and was a fervent supporter of the creation of the Offa's Dyke Path, being present at the opening ceremony and contributing a foreword to the official guidebooks. It is sometimes easy to forget nowadays, when mountaineers and tourists are queuing for their turn on the world's highest mountain, the excitement that greeted the news of that first successful climb of Mount Everest.

Eric Shipton, not John Hunt, was originally the intended leader of the Everest expedition. Shipton had done the preliminary reconnaissance and much of the other preparatory work and was miffed when the Everest Committee of the Alpine Club chose Hunt ahead of himself. Their reasoning was that Hunt, a very successful and distinguished army officer as well as a skilled mountaineer, was a better leader of men. One of the successful team said of him afterwards:

" What he achieved with us on Everest was that he had a group of prima donnas who all wanted to be the first to the top and he made us a team."

Those of you old enough will remember that the announcement of the successful ascent of the summit of Everest by Edmund Hillary and Sherpa Tenzing was announced on the same day as the coronation of Queen Brenda and was lauded as being a triumph for British guts as we entered the second Elizabethan Age. This was all rather odd, since Hillary was a New Zealander, Tenzing was a Nepalese, and they had reached the top three days before the actual coronation.

Half way up Llanfair Hill, where the Dyke stretches infinitely and wonderfully ahead, the Path is joined by the Jack Mytton Way, a long distance path that runs through some lovely parts of Shropshire. Now Mad Jack Mytton was a bit of a rum chap to say the least. Before he was fifteen he had been expelled from Harrow and Westminster, and for a year or two after that he lived at home, betting and drinking in inns, attending cockfights and races. He inherited the family wealth and used it to ill effect, building up stables of horses that he lavished huge bets on and entertaining his friends richly. He refused to accept responsibility for his behaviour, often deliberately irritating others, such as when he loosed a crate of four live foxes in the bar of Shrewsbury's Lion Hotel or when he ordered twenty pairs of skates and insisted on all his servants putting a pair on and taking to a frozen lake, while he stood laughing as they fell over. His wild ways soon spent up the family fortune and he ended up in debtors' prisons, where he died at the age of 38.

I must have been thinking about Jack Mytton's roguish life as I came down from Llanfair Hill, for I lost the path twice within the next two to three miles. It was raining heavily now and, despite wearing all the appropriate waterproofs, I could feel the rain seeping into my boots and sharp downhill descents on muddy paths were proving particularly treacherous. The Walkers' Guide was proving accurate about the switchback nature of this stretch of the Path and I couldn't really get into a comfortable stride pattern. Eventually I found my way pack on to the Path and the line of the Dyke just east of Newcastle where the Path crosses the River Clun on a wooden footbridge. From there it is a mere three miles eastwards to Clun itself.

Clunton and Clunbury,
Clungunford and Clun,
Are the quietest places
Under the sun.

So wrote A. E. Housman in his poem *A Shropshire Lad*, first published at the poet's own expense in 1896 and never out of print since, though I'm pretty sure most of its purchasers and readers know little about Housman himself or about the poem. And now you're dying to know, so I'll tease you no more.

Alfred Edward Housman was born near Bromsgrove in Worcestershire and not in Shropshire, which his poem describes, accurately in my opinion, as the "land of lost content", although there is evidence to suggest that he had only visited the county a couple of times before he wrote the poem by which he is now best remembered. A brilliant Classics scholar, Housman won a scholarship to Oxford where he met and fell in love with a fellow-student named Moses Jackson, a handsome athlete. Sadly, the affection was not reciprocated and some experts blame Housman's failure in his final examinations, when he handed in blank papers, on the emotional turmoil the future poet was experiencing. In 1882 he entered the patent office in London where Jackson was already working and moved into an apartment with Moses Jackson and his brother Adalbert but some years later Moses emigrated to India and married.

The distraught Housman threw himself into scholarly writing, with such success that in 1892 he was, remarkably considering his previous academic failure, appointed Professor of Greek and Latin at University College, London. *A Shropshire Lad* is a long set of 63 poems about unrequited love and loss, its subject almost certainly Moses Jackson, though when it was published no one recognised this. In the wake of the trial and subsequent imprisonment of Oscar Wilde, Housman was careful not to announce his own homosexuality, which only became widely known well after his death.

But, whether Housman had ever been there or not, is Clun one of the "quietest places under the sun"? It's a typically attractive border village of some 700 souls, with its atmospheric ruined castle, its old packhorse bridge connecting the Saxon side to the Norman side, and its Norman (and much-restored) church. It owes its position to its situation on the River Clun where the drovers would bring their flocks from Wales into England and it dates back long before the Saxons or Normans. If you walked through it in the middle of a summer's day, you would certainly call it quiet, maybe even sleepy.

But Clun has had its moments, for three of its citizens caused a proper rumpus in their lifetimes. At the time of the Norman invasion, the lands in this area belonged to Edric the Wild, known for his boozing and his hunting. One day, so the legend tells, while out hunting he came across six beautiful maidens (they always are, aren't they?) dancing round a seventh one that he fell instantly in love with and seized to take home as was his right as lord of the manor. This maiden was called Godda, the queen of the fairies, and she agreed to wed him as long as he never gave her a bollocking. So they lived happily ever after *et cetera et cetera*, until one day he told her off for being late with his breakfast boiled egg and toast soldiers. She vanished and Edric returned to his wild ways, hunting high and low for her unsuccessfully for the rest of his life. The Wild Hunt is one of the enduring tales of Britain; some say that it can be heard in the night sky foretelling war, the sound of Wild Edric blowing his horn in pursuit of the fairy Godda.

The Trinity almshouses in Clun were established by Henry Howard, the Earl of Northampton, allegedly in penance at his unwitting involvement in the Overbury affair at the time of James I. Howard's great niece Frances was married off at a tender age to Robert Devereux, the equally-young Earl of Essex, but, like many other arranged marriages of that time and this (cf. Charlie and Lady Di), it failed. Frances fancied the pants off the dashing Robert Carr and got hold of some poison to make Devereux impotent so that she could divorce him. Then Sir Thomas Overbury, Carr's mate who had actually been composing sonnets for Carr in praise of the scheming Frances, found out and threatened to expose her. So Fair Frances got Overbury imprisoned and poisoned him. Great Uncle Howard disposed of the evidence and voilà! Carr and Frances lived happily ever after. Until, that is, a servant revealed the truth and the pair were sent to trial with Anne Turner, Frances's accomplice, who was found guilty and hanged. Another player in this Jacobean drama was one Simon Forman, who provided the poisons and who was the model for the character Subtle in Ben Jonson's great play *The Alchemist*.

Curiously enough, another great playwright has even closer links with Clun. This is John Osborne, the creator of *Look Back in Anger*, the play that shook British drama out of its complacency in the 1950s and launched the literary movement known as the Angry Young Men. Osborne was the original Angry Young Man himself, who spent his life railing against the smugness and apathy of British society. He lived the latter part of his life here in Clun and is buried in the churchyard of St George's. The house he lived in is now owned by the Arvon Foundation and used as a place for aspiring writers to receive tuition from working writers. He would have appreciated that.

Quiet Clun may be but it houses some roistering ghosts.

The guys who built Offa's Dyke must have had a pretty horrific time on this stretch of the way, going sharply up hill and down dale, with no concessions to common sense. The Path and the actual Dyke coincide for a long distance here, which is when you appreciate the wondrousness of the engineering that created this monument, even though there are times when you wonder at your own sanity in choosing to walk along it. Up you go on to Hergan Hill, then down and up again to Middle Knuck, then down and up and steeply down again to Churchtown, where there is a church but no town. And then, just when you hope your legs have become attuned to this constant ascent and descent, there is one of the sharpest rises of all coming out of Churchtown and on to Edenhope Hill. I normally prefer to keep walking on an ascent but I have to say that on this particular climb I had to stop for breath at least four times. And just when you think you've cracked it, you're on the way down again alongside an imposing section of the Dyke to cross the River Unk via another footbridge and there ahead of you is the Dyke climbing once again through woods.

This was my lowest point of the day. It had been raining most of the day so far and the wet had penetrated my socks and boots, so that every footfall squelched. My legs ached from the constant dipping and rising, my dodgy left knee was threatening to reawaken, and any moment I expected the Achilles tendon on my right leg to start moaning in sympathy. I looked up at the Dyke as it made its ascent and I actually took my mobile phone out, thinking to ring my wife and ask her to come and rescue me. If I hadn't realised that it would have taken her longer to reach me than it would take me to climb up to the Kerry Ridgeway crawling backwards on hands and knees, I think I would have phoned. Instead I took a last sip of my water, that was running dangerously low by now, and, with still several miles to go to reach Montgomery, gritted my teeth and set to.

But that was it. Once I'd reached the Kerry Ridgeway, that old drovers' road across hilltops, it was all downhill and so, exhausted as I felt, it was doable. Passing from a field path on to a farm track I noticed a sign that announced Drewin Farm for accommodation. By now my water bottle was completely empty and, unsure what kind of a welcome I would get but actually not that bothered any longer as I was so desperate, I knocked on the front door. The farmer's wife, whose name is Ceinwen Richards, was kindness personified and took my water bottle willingly.

"Have you got time for a cup of tea?" she asked when she returned with my water. "There's tea in the pot because I've just made some for my neighbour."

Had I got time for a cup of tea? You betcha.

"That's very kind," I answered, trying to sound like a normal civilised human being rather than the exhausted lump of wobbling flesh I felt myself to be.

"Have you come far?"

"From Knighton. It's exhausting. It's all uphill and downhill."

"Yes, they all say that," she smiled. "Would you like a Welsh cake?"

Would I like a Welsh cake? Was this the kindest person in the whole universe? It was like seeing your mum when you came home from school.

"You've saved my life," I said. "My spirits were really down. Thank you. Let me pay you for this."

But she would take nothing and I left, reinvigorated and ready to believe that I could still do this walk. I strode off in the direction of the small village of Cwm and then, still following the actual Dyke itself, into the grounds of Mellington Hall which is now a hotel and whose grounds have been disfigured by one of the ugliest mobile home sites I have encountered. Prior to its current condition, Mellington Hall was the home of the Heap family, descendants of the rice importer Josiah Heap whose Diamond H Line of ships sailed out of Liverpool in the eighteenth and early nineteenth centuries. It was with the wealth from this trade that Sydney Rankin Heap bought Mellington Hall and shocked the local population by installing five bathrooms at a time when one was thought to be a luxury. He farmed an extensive 2000 acres and was active politically in the Montgomery area, becoming High Sheriff at one stage. His son, also called Sydney, was a great rowing champion and a member of the British team at the 1924 Paris Olympic Games.

Curiously, the Offa's Dyke Path emerges under the archway of the gatehouse to Mellington Hall and from then it was a steady trudge across fields with the Dyke as accompaniment, delayed by a sudden and ferocious thunderstorm from which I took shelter with some cows under a large oak tree. It was not long, however, before I was swinging away from the Dyke past the Montgomery Cricket Club's attractive ground in the parkland of Lymore, arriving in Montgomery itself at just six o'clock. It had been a long day's walk.

The second kind person I was to meet that day of twenty steaming wet miles was my landlady, Linda Whitticase at Llwyn House. Not only did she make me tea and offer me biscuits as soon as I arrived but she took my wet socks and boots off me and told me not to worry, as she'd have them dry by the morning. For some reason she'd been expecting two people and, while she went off to prepare my room for me, I was looked after by her daughter Sarah whose warm smile and chatty manner made me feel more human again. I sat on a comfy settee in a cosy room of an old house whose doors had been liberated from Montgomery Castle, so Linda Whitticase later told me, drinking tea and feeling as if I was one of the family. It was just what I needed.

That evening I didn't have to venture far as The Dragon Inn is situated just opposite Llwyn House and that's where I went for dinner. The Dragon is an old coaching house, dating back to the 16th century, full of old beams also allegedly liberated from Montgomery Castle. It is also unusual in having a swimming pool and sauna, for guests only of course. I felt I deserved a reward after the day's slog so lashed out on a spicy chicken dish that was delicious, a banana split with ice cream that was equally scrumptious, and ended with an Irish coffee. I replaced the liquid I had lost over the day with four pints of Wood's bitter.

I slept very, very well.

12 Montgomery

I wanted to call in at Montgomery because this lovely Georgian town contains within its environs virtually everything you might need to know about the history of this country. Too large a claim? Then consider the following.

The town lies on the historic trading route along the valley of the River Severn, so it's not too surprising to find relics from way way back. The ancient Brits were here. There's a prehistoric fort at Ffridd Faldwynn on a hillside half a mile west of the modern town centre. You have to say it's still pretty impressive to look at. Excavations have dated its origins to neolithic times but it was clearly used up to the Iron Age, when its Celtic occupants built massive earth ramparts reinforced by a timber frame as defences against incomers.

When the Roman legions arrived, they built a fort at The Gaer about a mile and a half away, to keep the Taffies at bay. Originally constructed in the second century, its defences enclosed an area of about 200 metres by 175 metres and it was laid out in standard Roman fashion, as used all over the Empire so their soldiers didn't get confused. (This is a bit like the way the modern American Empire builds MacDonald's restaurants all over the world so that its modern soldier-counterparts, i.e. tourists, don't feel too confused by the local grub.)

Offa, King of the Mercians, of course, built his dyke on the hillside just beyond the town to act as the border with the Welsh, though I've no idea if he popped into Montgomery looking for a Big Mac or a Double Cheeseburger.

Then there's the Ford of Montgomery at Rhydwhyman about a mile from the town. This was the spot where for centuries princes and kings, barons and bishops, knights and abbots met to sign treaties and patch up arguments, usually involving whether this bit was Welsh or not. Curiously enough, when the Cambrian railway was built through here, the level crossing here was named Rhydwhyman Crossing.

Roger de Montgomery, one of William the Conqueror's top men who looked after Normandy in 1066 while William was busy shooting arrows into Harold's eye, was given Shropshire for his loyalty and he gave the town its name. Actually Roger's motte and bailey castle was down by the riverside at Hendomen, commanding the natural approach from Shrewsbury and the valley of the River Camlad. The impressive castle ruins that are now visible on the hillside above the town square are from the time of Henry III, who built the first stone construction. The Castle is forever associated with the Herberts, of whom more anon, but its death knell was, as with so many castles, the Civil War, when in 1649 its demolition was ordered.

In 1536 Henry VIII made Montgomery the capital of the newly-created county of the same name and its present street layout owes its origins to that period, though many of its finest buildings in the wonderfully-wide Broad Street are of Georgian origin. It remained the county town until 1974, when Powys was created and the administrative headquarters of that county moved to neighbouring Welshpool. What remains now is this jewel of a town with its lovely buildings, its permanent peacefulness, and its abiding sense of having participated in much history but having decided now to watch everything unfolding elsewhere.

Okay, so now the Herbert family. Or the Herbies, as I like to think of them. This quintessential English family are nothing but phonies. The Herbert surname was adopted in the fifteenth century by the sons of one Sir William Thomas, allegedly because they thought it would forever link them to Herbert the Chamberlain, who was supposedly the illegitimate son of Henry I, and thus constitute their credentials as long-established scions of the aristocracy. There's more murkiness in the succession to the estates and titles but there is certainty that the Sir Richard Herbert buried in

Montgomery's church beneath a wonderfully-ornate stone canopy was the father of two extraordinary Herbies.

The first of these is George, the poet and clergyman, who was born in Montgomery Castle in 1593. After an early life of scholarship, he committed himself to the church and appears to have led an exemplary life, notably in his genuine kindness to the poor of his parish. He was a friend of John Donne and Izaak Walton, who later wrote a biography of him, but his poetry did not see the light of day until after his death. Apparently he gave the manuscript of his poems to a friend while on his deathbed and it was published privately soon afterwards. His work is commonly bracketed with that of John Donne and other metaphysical poets but, to tell the truth, since the collection was called *Sacred Poems and Private Ejaculations*, I think I ought to spare you the embarrassment. So instead here's a story about George Herbert when he was once taken ill.

He was taken to a Catholic hospital for coronary surgery. The operation went well, and as the groggy George regained consciousness, he opened his eyes to see a Sister of Mercy standing by his bed.

"Mr Herbert, you're going to be just fine," the nun said, patting his hand. "We do have to know, however, how you intend to pay for your stay here. Do you have insurance?"

"No," he whispered.

"Can you pay in cash?"

He shook his head slightly.

"Any close relatives?"

"Just my sister in Montgomery," George replied. "But she's a spinster nun."

"Nuns are not spinsters, Mr Herbert," said the nun firmly. "They are married to God."

"Fine," said George with a little smile. "Send the bill to my brother-in-law."

The second Herbie, George's brother Edward, was altogether a different kettle of fish. Born ten years earlier than his brother, Edward served abroad in the army before being made Ambassador in Paris, where he apparently spent more time duelling than conducting diplomatic affairs. We know all about this because he left a most amusing *Autobiography* describing his adventures in Paris and later London. Reading this, you can understand why later scholars believe that he had a very high opinion of himself. He claims, for instance, to have been introduced at the age of seventeen to Queen Elizabeth who, hearing that he was already married, remarked that this was regrettable, because she thought him a bit of top totty. He boasts of his brilliant success in curing the various ailments of himself, his children and his servants. He tells of the duels and rough-and-tumble street fights he was always engaging in and of the beautiful ladies who fell under his spell. In short, *The Autobiography* reads like it was written by a wannabe Jeffrey Archer. Here's a typical extract:

> *"When I came to Paris the English and French were in very ill intelligence with each other, insomuch that one Buckly coming then to me, said he was assaulted and hurt upon Pontneuf, only because he was an Englishman; nevertheless, after I had been in Paris about a month, all the English were so welcome thither, that no other nation was so acceptable among them."*

Get out the shepherd's pie and the Krug, eh?

This Herbie was involved in the final act of Montgomery Castle during the Civil War. Initially, Edward appeared to be supporting the king and the castle was seen as a royalist outpost, though he made excuses for not joining the royalist forces on two different occasions ("I've got a migraine" and "I've got another migraine"). A year later, however, Edward signed to surrender the castle to the Parliamentarians on condition that there was no violence. Red rag to a bull stuff that, of course. Within days a Royalist army had besieged the town and soon a mighty battle ensued. The result was a win for Cromwell's boys and in 1647, purely by chance of course, Edward was given the castle back. Sadly he died a year later and shortly after that the castle was demolished.

End of Montgomery Castle. End of the Herbies of Montgomery.

The good citizens of Montgomery have created their own rather wonderful museum in the Old Bell, formerly a sixteenth century inn. It is run entirely by volunteers and at the time of my visit only cost a quid to enter, which I think is excellent value. There are permanent exhibitions relating to the medieval and Norman castles and their archaeological excavations with excellent scale models of both. However, the room that most attracted my attention was one devoted to the Brynhyfred Workhouse, otherwise known in the euphemistic way of such things as the Forden House of Industry. This reminds you of how atrociously we used to treat some of the less fortunate members of our society. For instance, 'Blind Meg' Thomas was placed in the Poor Law Institution aged four as "mentally defective". She was blind, dumb and deaf but she could thread a needle and sew, and that's what she spent her life doing in Brynhyfred till her death aged 89. Imagine that, eighty-five years in an institution! And, just in case you think I'm talking about ancient history, let me point out that the last patient left Brynhyfred as recently as 1997.

The old workhouse at Brynhyfred has been rebadged as Camlad House and it is now the home of the Universal Confluence of Yoga-Vedanta Luminary (U.C.Y.L) and its activities. These include Yoga and Vedanta classes, spiritual discourses, meditation days and residential weekends, youth programmes, Hatha Yoga classes and Hatha Yoga teachers' training courses.

Now you either buy into all this sort of thing or you don't. Yoga supposedly helps you to stop your mind from wandering. It improves your perception and helps you to understand your own mind and senses. It helps control stress and strain and stops internal conflicts and confusions. Above all it helps you to understand the truth and takes you to peace, happiness and self-knowledge. Or so they say. Personally I find good beer does the business.

Camlad House is also the home of The Order Of Wandering Peace Poets, of the International Institute of Peace Studies and Global Philosophy, and of the Green University. Just to give you a flavour of some of this, here's a bit about the Wandering Peace Poets:

> *Through poetry, and the fellowship of the inspired word,*
> *through music and song, and through the study of the world's*
> *diverse poetic traditions, we believe that peace and harmony*
> *can be restored to earth, and that we can pull back from the*
> *brink of the collective follies affecting our current century*
> *and generation.*

Tell that to George Dubya!

All of these organisations are led by one Thomas Daffern, who was also responsible for establishing the Truth and Reconciliation Commission for Stonehenge, "so that a solution to the problems of the Solstice celebrations can be found in terms of a just compromise that recognises the legitimate needs of all parties".

Is this the man who will save the world?

When Don MacLean penned the lyrics to *American Pie*, I'm pretty sure he wasn't thinking of what his words meant to me. MacLean was, of course, writing about what he called "the day the music died", which we all now know was 3rd February 1959, when the light aircraft carrying rock n' roll legend Buddy Holly crashed a few minutes after take-off from the small airport of Mason City in Iowa, killing all those on board. What those words signified to me was not the death of rock n' roll but the death of my teenage dream of wearing large horn-rimmed specs à la Buddy Holly. Really!

What kind of sad adolescence did I have!

Well, I suppose the attraction of Buddy Holly was that he was not Elvis. I mean, he didn't do all that macho posturing and sexual gyrating of the hips that the King was famous for. Instead Buddy just stood on stage and sang, grinning at us through the TV screen underneath those huge horn-rimmed glasses. He gave hope to all us wannabe rock n' rollers who were rather geeky in appearance and gauche in manner. Throughout my teenage years, I really thought that, rather like Clark Kent transmuting into Superman by removing his glasses, I could do the business in reverse by adopting horn-rimmed glasses to make me irresistible to the opposite sex and the object of envy to my mates. The only problem with this was that my eyesight was A1 OK so it had to remain a forlorn dream, which 3rd February 1959 took away from me.

Of course, we had a horn-rimmed hero closer to home in Hank Marvin, guitarist with Cliff Richard's backing band The Shadows. But at that time The Shadows were mere bit players to Cliff's sultry angst-ridden impersonation of James Dean. It wasn't until 1960, a year after "the day the music died", that they bumped into Jerry Lordan, also trying to make it in rock n' roll, and he offered them the tune to *Apache* which was to be the band's first Number 1 hit.

Jerry Lordan, until his death from liver failure in 1995, lived in a cottage just outside Montgomery, though hardly anyone in the town knew who he was. Before he died, he recalled an interesting moment during the recording of *Apache* at the Abbey Road studios in London:

This is Studio Two at Abbey Road, so there's a huge props room under the stairs stuffed full of cowbells and you name it, and they came out with this Chinese drum. It's actually called a tam tam, and it's circular with a rope on it, and you hold it in one hand and beat with a mallet with the other, and Cliff Richard held that over Tony Meehan's drum kit... That's him all the way through, bom bom bom bom, bom bom... he kept great time, too.

So there you have it, a moment in pop history encapsulated forever - Cliff Richard playing percussion on the record that curiously enough was to displace his own record at the top of the charts. *Apache* has been publicly performed and played, literally, millions of times. In fact, shortly before his death, Jerry Lordan received an award for one million American performances. He wrote many other tunes that became hit records - *Wonderful Land* and *Mustang* for the Shadows, *Diamonds* for ex-Shadow Jet Harris, as well as minor hits for Cliff Richard and Shane Fenton (who later became Alvin Stardust). There must be hundreds of late-middle-aged men who tried to emulate the haunting sounds of *Apache* and *Diamonds* on their cheap nineteen-fifties guitars. Some of them, I guess, turned into Eric Clapton, George Harrison, Ronnie Wood *et cetera*. Others, no doubt, became civil servants and bank managers but hey! that's life.

It was curious to be recalling this lost era and my foolish desire to be kitted out in horn-rimmed spectacles, while visiting this even older town of Montgomery on the Welsh borderland.

13 Montgomery to Oswestry

Ah, the wonders of sleep! Next morning I was bright and cheery again, aches and pains forgotten, socks washed and dried, boots no longer squelchy, ready for the off. I was profuse in my thanks to Linda Whitticase, because being accepted into the homely atmosphere of Llwyn House had done much to restore my spirits and her excellent breakfast did the rest. Soon I had rejoined the Offa's Dyke Path, still following the clear green outline of the Dyke itself, where it acts to this day as the boundary between England and Wales. Everything was wet underfoot but, at least when I started walking, the rain held off, though the weather forecast promised more precipitation as the day wore on.

The Path takes you on a footbridge over the fast-flowing River Camlad, the only river that rises in England then flows into Wales. This is a mystical area and one where legend has it that Arthur fought his last battle. The evidence for this is in *The Mabinogion* (remember *The Red Book of Hergest?*) in a tale called *The Dream of Rhonabwy*, written in about1150. The tale is set in Powys on the eve of the Battle of Camlann, which you have to admit does sound suspiciously like Camlad. Arthur is rallying his men at a river crossing at Rhyd-y-Groes that can still be seen today, where it is marked by Shiregrove Bridge, about a mile east of the Dyke. According to that great storyteller Geoffrey of Monmouth, the Battle of Camlann was Arthur's final battle, possibly fought in 520. Arthur was, as you will no doubt recall, mortally wounded in this battle and ordered his knight Bedivere to take his sword Excalibur and throw it into the lake. When he did so, the Lady of the Lake's arm rose from the depths, caught the sword and took it down into the water. And Arthur was then mysteriously transported to Avalon to become the source of a million romantic myths.

Altogether now, aah!

Leaving Arthur's battlefield, through moist fields and woods now, the Dyke marches on till it becomes part of the old Roman Road across the Long Mountain, before leaving the road and entering Leighton Woods. The lengthy forest track eventually brings you out below a hill on which the Iron Age Beacon Ring is situated. Just as I was about to start climbing, the heavens opened again and I quickly donned my full rain gear.

Beacon Ring was built about 2500 years ago. It is a roughly circular enclosure within an earth bank. The community that settled there would have built a small village of round wooden houses in the middle of the enclosure. A gap in the encircling bank shows where an entrance would have been, which would have been closed by a wooden gate. The inside of the fort was planted with woodland in 1953 to mark Elizabeth II's coronation and from the air the initials ER can be picked out, which was not a lot of use to me walking. The utilities have commandeered this spot, however, and there is a radio mast and a covered reservoir in the middle of this ancient site. From the top of Beacon Ring there are good views down the valley to Welshpool, but I had no intention of calling in there.

There was then a steady descent, still in rain and through high-cropped footpaths across fields down to the River Severn itself at Buttington and then, escaping from the noisy main road, along the quiet towpath of the Montgomery Canal to reach Pool Quay, where I had planned to have my lunch at the Powis Arms.

I had phoned ahead to check that the Powis Arms was indeed open at lunchtime, only to be assured by the landlord, who I now know to be called Alan, that it never closed. When I walked in, damp and wearing half a field of wheat, little did I know what I was to find. There were four other blokes in the bar - a tall bearded guy in smart casual clothes, two road labourers of uncertain age, and Alan the landlord. Let me start with him because he is the hero of this piece. He was sat by an unlit fire, with several days' stubble adorning his chin and with his zimmer frame placed before him for convenience. I later learned that he had had a stroke.

"Are you the one that rang this morning?" he asked in a strong Scouse twang.

"Yes, that's me," I said, grinning with pleasure that I had been so recognised.

"What d'you want to drink?" he asked.

I looked at the selection of beers on display and asked for a pint of shandy.

"You pull it," Alan instructed the tall bearded guy, who looked a little surprised but, no doubt recognising Alan's physical difficulties, did as requested.

I downed the shandy quickly and asked for a further pint of Brains bitter.

"D'you like real ale, then?" asked Alan. "If you do, you don't want Brains, that's keg. You want to try Doctor Duncan. It's good. Cain's brewery. From Liverpool. Real good. Real ale."

"Okay," I said. "I'll go with that. Pint of Doctor Duncan, whoever he might be."

"Medical Officer of Health in Liverpool back then," Alan retorted. "The world's first ever Medical Officer of Health."

It was becoming clear to me that what I had stumbled on was a little corner of Scouseland in the middle of Wales. I looked around the room and saw further evidence in the shape of newspaper photographs of Bill Shankly, Liverpool F.C.'s greatest manager, and Kenny Dalgleish, one of their greatest ever players. Plus the scarf, plus the Liverpool clock, plus all the other memorabilia that only a true Liverpool nut would collect.

"Aye, we've had some great beers here, haven't we? D'you remember that Skull Attack? That did just what it said. We've had some bad heads with that, haven't we?" Alan reminisced, talking now to the tall bearded guy, who it turned out worked for the wonderful independent wine merchant Tanner's, whose warehouse is in Welshpool and who have a shop in my home town of Bridgnorth.

"Alan, I'll leave this with you," said the man from Tanner's, passing a small parcel to him. "I have to go now. I'll see you next week. Look after yourself."

And he left.

"You'll be sorry to see Liverpool losing to Wolves this year then," I said, resuming the conversation though mostly in jest, for my team Wolverhampton Wanderers had only just succeeded in getting into the Premier League for the first time ever.

Alan grinned through his stubble.

"I remember going to Molineux for the last match of the season back in the 1970s," he reminisced again. "D'you remember it? Crucial it was for both sides. We had to win to get the championship and Wolves had to win to stay in the First Division. It was heaving there that night. It was a brilliant night."

"Who won?" I asked.

"We did, of course," he snorted. "Who d'you think, lad?"

I haven't been called 'lad' for a good number of years now and was about to point my age out to him when one of the road-builders stood and asked if he and his pal could have another round of drinks.

"Yeah, just go and pull them yourselves," said Alan, not even trying to shift from his seat. "And give me the money."

"Do you want a drink yourself?" asked the road-builder, now pulling himself a fresh pint of lager.

"No, it's too soon to start just yet," replied Alan. "Me and Scotty usually get started after everybody's left at night. We'll probably have nine or ten pints before we go to bed."

By this time I had drained my own pint and, much as I was tempted by the pleasure of Alan's company to stay longer, I knew I had some miles to go before I reached my night's resting place. So, I fastened up my cagoule, pulled my rucksack on to my shoulders and said my goodbyes. I kind of loved this notion of a pub where the landlord does the entertaining but the customers pull the pints, especially when the landlord was as unconventional a character as Alan was. I left much cheered.

The afternoon's walking followed a route that was familiar to me, along the floodbanks of the River Severn. The Offa's Dyke Path and the Severn Way converge hereabouts for about five miles, until the Path heads north on to a short section of the Dyke. The walk went through the soaking fields, past herds of grazing cattle who stared liquidly at me but, no doubt seeing my walking pole, decided against any precipitate action. On occasion, where cows were sat on the line of the path in front of a stile, I had to wave my pole and shout "Bugger Offa!"

But such occasions were rare and there was even a little watery sunshine in the late afternoon as I approached the end of another day's long walk. The walking was easy, except for one tiny stretch through Gornel Farm where the Path has been churned up into a thick quagmire by regular cattle activity and where two yapping dogs sought to discourage me from following the waymarked route. I don't know if the pole helped but I waved it at them menacingly, muttered "Bugger Offa!" at them and continued into Four Crosses

Ced and Jill Deathridge, who keep the Golden Lion in Four Crosses where I stayed that night, are from Birmingham and I immediately felt at home. Ced is a big, outgoing, jovial man with a big grin for everyone, while Jill is warm and cheerful and just as helpful.

"Take your shoes and socks off here," were her first words, "and give me all your wet stuff. I'll hang it up in the drying room and it'll be fine by the morning. And if you've got anything else you need drying, just chuck it down the stairs and I'll deal with it."

She showed me to my room, made arrangements for breakfast and left me to it.

"I'm a yam yam," said Ced by way of introduction, when I went downstairs for an early evening pint. He was behind the bar sorting out a raffle but had obviously discovered that I originated in the Black Country. "You'm a yow yow."

"Sort of," I agreed. "What brings you here, though? In the middle of Wales?"

"The land," he replied. "I've built five holiday cottages since we've been here. And now I'm building a house for us to retire to."

"We're retiring this year," said Jill, who appeared from nowhere. "Well, that's what he says. But I expect we'll end up doing something else."

"How come?" I quizzed her.

"I know him," she said, giving him a glance that said a lot.

"I don't believe in doing nothing," Ced explained. "I was out in the Middle East for years but, when we came back, I was clearly an embarrassment to the company, so I took redundancy and retired at fifty. Then I got bored, so I started my own business and ran that for ten years, then I retired again."

"Then we took on the pub," said Jill, giving him that glance again.

"Do you get a lot of walkers from the Dyke staying here?" I asked.

"Yes, we used to, though not so many in the last couple of years," Ced replied. "Since foot and mouth. I lost a lot of customers that year and I didn't get much compensation from the government either."

"Really?"

Ced nodded and turned to serve a new customer at the bar, while I gave Jill my order for dinner and for another pint of Speckled Hen. When I looked again, Ced had disappeared.

"He's playing out," Jill explained.

"What do you mean?"

"On the new house. They're putting in fence posts, I think. He can't leave it alone. But, if he doesn't get back in here soon, you're not going to get your dinner. I'll call him."

She did, and not long afterwards I enjoyed my *boeuf bourgignon* and a further pint of bitter, before heading off towards my bedroom.

Ced was back at the bar by now

"You off to bed then? Have we put the world to rights?"

I grinned and said goodnight. In truth, when you're in the company of people like Ced, you do believe that you can put the world to rights. Even though deep down in your heart you know it will probably still carry on in its normal unsteady way forever.

Next day, Wednesday, the weather had picked up and, once more in dried socks and boots, I set off from Four Crosses, quickly joining the towpath of the Montgomery Canal again for two miles until it reached Llanymynech, where I suddenly realised I had left my gaiters back at the Golden Lion. I didn't want to tempt the rain gods, so rang back and Ced, bless him, drove up to meet me and return the mislaid articles. Then it was up a steep hill on to Llanymynech golf course, one of the few courses designed by the legendary six-times Open Champion Harry Vardon, where a strange figure appeared ahead of me, waving feebly in my direction. On closer inspection the figure turned out to be an ageing female, who wore a smock over baggy pants and boots while on her head she had a Bill and Ben floppy hat.

"Do you know the way?" she asked. "I think I'm lost."

She spoke in an American accent and I soon found out that she was from New York.

"Where are you going?" I asked.

"Aren't you doing the Offa's Dyke Path?" she queried, obviously under the assumption that anyone wearing hiking gear in Britain must be walking the said Path that she was undertaking.

"Of course I am," I answered. "What's the problem?"

"I keep going round in circles."

To be fair, the Path was a little overgrown around here, as you skirt the westward side of the golf course and head into the Llanymynech Nature Reserve that has been created from the no-longer-used quarry. But it wasn't that difficult and we were soon on our way, though I suspected her inquiry was more to do with seeking companionship than with being genuinely lost. I was stuck with her.

"Why are you doing this walk?" she quizzed, as we fought our way through the bracken.

I told her about the book I was planning.

"And why are you doing it?" I continued.

"I'm on a journey," she replied, doing that strange thing with two fingers of each hand that really sad people do to indicate quotation marks.

My heart sank. I really wanted to get on with my journey, not to listen to her psychobabble.

"Oh," I sad non-committally, hoping that my lack of enthusiasm might put her off. It didn't.

"I've just had the most dreadful year," she added. "It's been an absolute nightmare. I'm in the middle of a divorce. I knew I just had to get away. My therapist told me I needed to go on a journey to clear my head."

"Couldn't you have just caught a plane somewhere?" I said. "Why are you putting yourself through all this?"

I was showing my irritation, I know, but by now it had become obvious that she couldn't read a map properly and had let some organisation arrange her overnight stays so haphazardly that one day she had to cover twenty-five miles, while the next day was only six or seven miles long.

"I wanted to do a proper journey," she answered, doing that irritating gesture with her fingers again. "A journey where the physical was married to the spiritual and I could find my real self again."

Oh shit! I thought. A complete American nutter. And I was walking with her.

"Which do you prefer, Offa's Dyke South or Offa's Dyke North?" she quizzed me.

"I wasn't aware there was a competition," I answered, thinking how stupid this line of questioning was.

"I think I prefer the South," she went on. "It was much more interesting. I think the political dimension of the Path is interesting, don't you? I think they're trying to promote Offa as a European king, because of his links with Charlemagne and the foreign trading, so they can get hold of some European Union money. What do you think?"

I hadn't thought about this far-fetched idea at all, though I suppose it makes some kind of sense.

"Did you stop in Hay-on-Wye?" she asked next.

"Yes, I love it there."

"Did you meet Richard Booth?" she asked.

"No," I said. "Though I'd love to have been there when he proclaimed himself King of Hay."

"I was out in the Far East in my younger days and I remember being in Delhi when I'd just got engaged," she said, in an apparently unconnected aside. "And a young man I met there sent me a huge bunch of red roses which I had to dispose of because of my fiancé. It was nearly very embarrassing. When I interviewed Richard twenty years later, he didn't recognise me."

"It was Richard Booth who sent you the roses?" I asked incredulously. "What was he doing in India?"

"Yes, it was him," she replied. "His wife's called Hope, you know. And that's my name too."

I don't know if any of this is true or not. In fact, I wasn't sure whether she was real or a figment of my imagination. By now we had slowly dragged ourselves to Nantmawr, where she had told me she was staying that night. Although it was only eleven o'clock in the morning, she had a book to read, she told me.

"A book about a journey?" I teased her.

But irony is not Americans' strong suit.

"No," she answered with a straight face. "It's a book about maps."

I left hopeless Hope outside the bungalow in Nantmawr where she was staying. She had walked five miles and that was her day over. I had a bit further to go to reach Oswestry.

There is another sharp climb coming out of Nantmawr on the way up a mountain called Moelydd but before you reach the summit you have to go through an enchanting piece of woodland known as Jones's Rough, now maintained by the Shropshire Wildlife Trust but a place with an interesting history. Just before you enter the wood stands a cottage known as Mount Zion. This was erected by a family called Jones without permission, based on their belief in old folklore which states that, if there was smoke coming from the chimney by morning, the builders could claim the dwelling as their home. The woodland alongside the cottage was only suitable for subsistence farming, though kindling was collected there for the bread oven that still exists at Mount Zion, hazel nuts were gathered in the autumn to sell in Oswestry market, and moss was collected to make wreaths.

Some life, eh? And some life also for the Pearl-bordered Fritillary butterfly, a protected species found in Jones's Rough. The Pearl-bordered Fritillary is a gorgeous brown- and orange-patterned butterfly, with little blobs of white and black on its wings, that used to be common throughout Britain but that has declined seriously in the past century, particularly in more recent times. Already it is extinct in Eastern England and it is threatened elsewhere because of changes in the management of woodlands. Jones's Rough is one of four sites in Shropshire where this highly scarce species of butterfly can be found.

Now why does this matter? Why should we seek to preserve species that are dying out? Who cares about the odd butterfly, except the odd (very odd) butterfly collector? Does biodiversity really improve the planet or is it all based on some romantic notions of saving everything because we feel guilty for having destroyed so many species unwittingly in the past?

I was thinking thus as I climbed up to the summit of Moelydd from where the views on what was becoming a really pleasant day were quite stunning, looking west to the Berwyn Mountains and south to the Long Mynd. And I was still pondering on these matters when I reached the Efel Inn at Trefonen, where I stopped for lunch. As I gazed at my coronation chicken sandwich, I began to ask myself questions about chicken farming and other forms of forced feeding that we as a species perpetrate on other species in order to feed and clothe ourselves.

And what about those contented-looking bullocks I had recently passed in a field on the Path? Were they any happier because they could wander freely around a grassy meadow and eat as much grass as possible than the battery hen who had been fed, plucked and killed in order to provide my lunch?

We just don't know, do we? Do cows have feelings? Do sheep long to shag rather than to be cloned? Do turkeys ever vote for Christmas? And would the fate of the Pearl-bordered Fritillary butterfly really bother me in six months time?

I chewed in thoughtful silence.

Mid-afternoon I arrived in Oswestry, entering past Oswestry School and then finding my lodging for the night. Later I went on a short tour of the town in the early evening sunlight, watching in amusement the failed tricks of the skateboarding youths in the war memorial park before finding the Railway Tavern for a cooling drink. The place was choc-a-bloc full of workmen, some of whom wore T-shirts that proclaimed 'Men on Top'. I thought they must be some kind of Oswestry response to feminism but it turned out they were roofers and tilers. It was clearly thirsty work for in the short period I was there, each of them consumed three pints of Guinness and they all smoked cigarettes as if they had gone out of fashion.

Later still I decided to go for a curry, since Oswestry was the largest of the towns on my journey and was, I thought, likely to have a reasonable supply of curry houses. The one I chose was the Simla Tandoori Restaurant, established 1971, prop: M. Shiah, who served me himself and was very punctilious in ensuring I had all I wanted, even to the point of offering help with one or two of *The Guardian* crossword clues that I was attempting. As the evening progressed, it became clear that this was one of the favourite haunts of the Oswestry middle class and I had the misfortune to have four of them sit at a table immediately adjacent to mine. As their loud conversation spewed through the room, I worked out that the foursome comprised a teacher from a local independent school, his wife who was the school nurse, a local farmer and his wife. Let me give you a flavour of their conversation, peppered as it was with unsavoury *bon mots*.

"Selwyn Gummer was excellent. That was a high point for British agriculture." (Farmer)

"Good manners are important in how you take a joke." (Teacher)

"I was disappointed with Athens. Too many dogs about. And all that 1950s architecture." (Farmer's wife)

"He's done well for a second-rater." (Farmer)

"You can't say that sort of thing nowadays, of course. It's not PC." (Teacher)

"Went on a counselling course and they're always the same.

Had to tell someone I'd never met before the worst thing that had ever happened to me. Well, you don't, do you? I made something up." (School nurse)

And so on and so forth. You can write the rest yourself. It was the kind of middle-class braying I dislike intensely.

Though I have to say the curry was excellent and M.Shiah did provide me, unwittingly, with the answer to one of the crossword clues.

11 across: Snake-ale (5)

Answer: Cobra (I drank two bottles of it).

14 Oswestry

I've been avoiding Oswestry most of my life and I'm not unusual in having done so. Those wonderful folk whose job it is to provide routes for traffic through urban areas have taken it upon themselves to steer you around Oswestry ever since I can remember with a variety of alternative and by-pass routes. The latest of these is their finest yet, as it takes you, on what used to be known as Watling Street when the Romans were driving their chariots up and down here, right round the outside of the town altogether, so that all you can see of Oswestry proper are a few grey roofs.

This is all a great pity because, though its centre has, like those of the majority of British towns, suffered from the depredations of town planners in thrall to the mighty internal combustion engine and the financial lures of the national retail trade, much remaining to recommend it. There's the Castle Mound, for instance - the nicely-maintained site of the Norman castle whose strategic importance was once great but which was destroyed during the Civil War. There's the greystone Guildhall of late Victorian origin but done in an ornate French Renaissance style with the town crest featuring the legendary King Oswald (of whom more anon). And more recently, but just as fascinatingly, there's the 1980s Festival Square whose centrepiece is a rather wonderful statue of the Borderland Farmer, the work of locally-born sculptor Ivor Robert Jones, whose statue of Winston Churchill graces Parliament Square in London. I'm told that many local farmers hate this representation because it is too belligerent looking, though others claim that it is very true to life!

Then there's the gorgeous timber-framed Llwyd Mansion right in the centre of town - the family residence of the Llwyd family who were very central to the development of Oswestry. The family included Edward Llwyd who became Keeper of the Ashmolean Museum in Oxford in 1691 and was much involved in developing an understanding of Welsh history, archaeology and language. There are also, as is not uncommon in such old market towns, a large number of pubs, so many in fact that some residents believe the town has more pubs per head of population than anywhere else in the United Kingdom. One of these, and one of the oldest at that, is the Wynnstay Hotel, at various times in the past known as the Cross Foxes or The Bowling Green and quite clearly in that great tradition of coaching inns to serve travellers on the old Watling Street, before it was diverted away from the town centre.

One of the most attractive buildings is the old grammar school, which claims to be the second oldest grammar school in England, founded in 1407 when its pupils would have studied the longbow in addition to Latin and mathematics, and is now the Oswestry Heritage Centre. Here you can find exhibitions of work by local artists and craftspeople, displays by schools and local societies, and - glory of glories - the award-winning Shropshire Poacher Coffee Shop. The Head Poacher is a glamorous lady with lustrous ginger hair and a wicked sense of humour and it was she who took my order and shortly afterwards returned with what I can only describe as a culinary triumph - tasty Columbian coffee and a salmon and crab sandwich which oozed with flavour. I half wished I'd arrived earlier for the menu presented appetising lunchtime alternatives - rogan josh with rice and salad and mango chutney, Welsh lamb and leek pie, Spanish omelettes, Shropshire pie *et cetera*, *et cetera*.

The Heritage Centre also houses the local tourist information base where a very helpful lady told me of the long-standing rivalry that had existed between Oswestry and Shrewsbury in their desire to be the leading wool-trading town. From her I also learned how the town got its name after the battle of Maserfeld in 642 A.D. when the Mercian king Penda - one of Offa's great ancestors - defeated the Northumbrian king Oswald and ordered that Oswald's corpse should be hung on a tree, thus giving the place its name of Oswald's Tree.

But the best piece of information I got at the Heritage Centre was about one of its former alumni - one William Spooner, who was a pupil at the Grammar School in Victorian times and who is, of course, the man responsible for that piece of verbal dexterity known as a spoonerism. In this linguistic somersault *a well-oiled bicycle* becomes *a well-boiled icicle, conquering kings* become *kinkering kongs,* and *slips of the tongue* become *tips of the slung.*

William Archibald Spooner was an unusual-looking man, born an albino with poor eyesight and a head too large for his body. Nevertheless he was an outstanding scholar and, after his time at Oswestry Grammar School, he began a sixty-year association with New College in Oxford. After completing his studies, he became a lecturer in history, philosophy and divinity, and from 1903 to 1924 was Warden. He was apparently very absent-minded and once invited a lecturer at New College to tea in order to meet the new Fellow in Archaeology.

"But I am the new Fellow in Archaeology," protested the man, whose name was Casson.

"Never mind," said Spooner. "Come all the same."

On another occasion, after preaching a long sermon one Sunday, he looked up at his student congregation and said:

"In the sermon I have just preached, whenever I said Aristotle, I meant St Paul."

And in another sermon he allegedly launched the following spoonerism:

"Which of us has not felt in his heart a half-warmed fish?"

Another time, when officiating at a wedding, he said to a hesitant bridegroom:

"Son, it is now kisstomary to cuss the bride."

And once, on the occasion of some royal success or other, he raised a toast to Her Majesty Queen Victoria with the following words:

"Three cheers for our queer old dean!"

But my favourite is this series of spoonerisms used in a rebuke to a badly behaved student:

"You have tasted a whole worm. You have hissed my mystery lectures. You were fighting a liar in the quadrangle. You will leave by the town drain."

Now I don't believe that anyone could be so verbally infelicitous and there is some evidence to suggest that many of these spoonerisms were student inventions but they no doubt echoed this unfortunate habit of their inventor. Spooner, however, had the misfortune to have to live with the fact that he would be remembered forever by crossword compilers and other students of linguistic matters for this habit. The term spoonerism was actually included in the Oxford English Dictionary of 1919 - eleven years before Spooner himself died.

I don't know how you cope with something like that and I don't expect I shall ever have to. But poor old Spooner, the child of Oswestry Grammar School, will always be remembered not for the worthy life he led but for the verbal slips he may or may not have made.

Sod rest his goal.

Oswestry's most famous son is the outstanding poet of the First World War, Wilfred Owen, who was born in a house called Plas Wilmot not far from the centre of town in 1893. Plas Wilmot is quite a posh house and is currently occupied by local doctors, who do nothing to encourage rubberneckers like myself to see over the high walls. And anyway, what's the point? There is a curiosity factor at play in us all, I guess, which is why we periodically traipse around places where famous people were born or once lived. But really, does a visit to Haworth Parsonage really give you much insight into the troubled and turbulent minds of the Brontë sisters (or of Kate Bush)? Does the tour of Ann Hathaway's Cottage really tell you anything about her husband, the ineffable Will Shakespeare? And would we really feel greater empathy with the soldiers who lived and died in the mud-filled trenches of France if we could get inside Plas Wilmot?

Still, Wilfred Owen was born here and his tragic story bears retelling. As I said, Plas Wilmot was a reasonably well-to-do property; belonging to the poet's grandfather but on the latter's death the family fortunes disintegrated. Owen's father worked in the railways and the family decamped first to Birkenhead and then some time later to Shrewsbury. An exhibition in the Oswestry Heritage Centre displays, alongside copies of the poet's birth certificate and photographs, a copy of a letter written by Susan Owen about her beloved son:

"He was always a very thoughtful, imaginative child...not very robust, and never cared for games. As a little child his greatest pleasure was for me to read to him even after he could himself."

There is no doubt that he was inordinately close to his mother and wrote to her on a very regular basis about what he was doing. His letters from the battlefields tell us much about his state of mind and provide illuminating commentaries on his poetry.

After school he became a parish assistant and there were hopes that he might enter the clergy. He tried to go to university but failed his examinations and instead went to France where he took a job as a teacher of English at a Berlitz school of languages. At this time he was writing poetry in the style of John Keats - romantic and flowery - and there was no sign of the poet he was to become.

Then in 1915 he returned home and signed up for the army, where he was enlisted in the Artists' Rifles. It would be hard to think of a more unsuitable name for a fighting unit, wouldn't it? Be that as it may, Owen was shipped out to France at the end of 1916 and for the next few months was in and out of the front line where the fighting was at its fiercest. The horrors were immediately apparent to him. To his mother he wrote:

"I can see no excuse for deceiving you about these 4 days. I have suffered seventh hell. I have not been at the front. I have been in front of it."

There is no doubt that Owen suffered himself as well as witnessing the suffering of others. On one occasion he was entombed in a cellar for thirty-six hours after falling through the floor of the building. On another occasion, a shell exploded near his head, threw him into the air and he spent the next few days in a hole covered with corrugated iron. As a result of this latter experience, Owen was diagnosed as suffering from shell-shock and was sent to Craiglockhart in Scotland to recuperate after having borne witness "to not a sign of life on the horizon and a thousand signs of death". It was there that he met Siegfried Sassoon, and his life changed.

Sassoon was an established poet who had been sent to Craiglockhart because he had written a letter to his colonel protesting about the wickedness of the war and the unnecessary suffering that the soldiers were enduring because of the crassness of the political and military leaders. The letter began thus:

"I am making this statement as an act of wilful defiance of military authority, because I believe that the war is being deliberately prolonged by those who have the power to end it."

By rights Sassoon should have been court-martialled for this act of defiance but thanks to the intervention of his fellow-poet Robert Graves, who served in the same battalion, he was sent to Craiglockhart reputedly suffering, like Owen, from shell shock.

As well as being a published poet, Sassoon knew many in the fashionable literary circles of London. Having befriended Owen and taken a liking to his poems, he introduced his young protégé to people like H.G. Wells and Robert Graves himself. He also encouraged Owen to explore the symptoms of shell shock - flashbacks, recurrent and repetitive nightmares, and his inability to escape from memories of battle - within his poetry.

In September 1917 Owen rejoined his regiment but was not sent back to France until midway through the following year. In between he wrote profusely and the poems of that period are what now provide us with such awful pictures of that terrible conflict. In September Owen participated in a front-line action for which he was awarded the Military Cross. In November, a few days before the end of the war, Owen and his fellow soldiers took refuge from German shelling in the cellar of a destroyed house, where he wrote this letter to his mother:

"Dearest Mother,

So thick is the smoke in this cellar that I can hardly see by a candle 12 inches away. And so thick are the inmates that I can hardly write for pokes, nudges, and jolts. On my left, the company commander snores on a bench. It is a great life. I am more oblivious than the less, dear mother, of the ghastly glimmering of the guns outside and the hollow crashing of the shells.

I hope you are as warm as I am, soothed in your room as I am here. I am certain you could not be visited by a band of friends half so fine as surround us here. There is no danger down here - or if any, it will be well over before you read these lines..."

How wrong he was. Two days later Owen was shot in action and killed. The telegram informing his parents of his death arrived on November 11th, the day the signing of the Armistice ended the war, when the church bells of Oswestry rang out for peace.

If in some smothering dreams, you too could pace
Behind the wagon that we flung him in,
And watch the white eyes writhing in his face,
His hanging face, like a devil's sick of sin,
If you could hear, at every jolt, the blood
Come gargling from the froth-corrupted lungs
Bitter as the cud
Of vile, incurable sores on innocent tongues,—
My friend, you would not tell with such high zest
To children ardent for some desperate glory,
The old Lie: Dulce et decorum est
Pro patria mori.

So ends one of Wilfred Owen's greatest and most memorable poems. It is a lesson the world still has not learned.

Oswestry has the unusual distinction of being the home of another well-known writer, Barbara Pym, who spent the first twenty years of her life here in a house not far from that in which Wilfred Owen was born. Now I have to say that, until I came to visit the town I had never read anything by Barbara Pym. In fact, I had barely heard of her. So I had to do some digging to find out about her and then to read something she had written. For otherwise my credibility with you, dear reader, would be zilch, eh?

Barbara Pym was born in 1913. Her father was a solicitor and her mother was the organist at St Oswald's parish church. Barbara read English at Oxford, worked for the Censorship Office in Bristol in the early years of the Second World War and later joined the Women's Royal Navy. After the war she went to work for the International African Institute in London, and soon became the assistant editor for the journal *Africa*. All this time she was writing and even submitted stories for women's magazines, but without success. More significantly, she submitted her first novel to the publisher Jonathan Cape in 1949 and *Some Tame Gazelle* was published in 1950, to favourable reviews.

From then on every few years a new Pym novel was produced. *Excellent Women* was published in 1952, followed in 1953 by *Jane and Prudence, Less than Angels* in 1955, *A Glass of Blessings* in 1958, and *No Fond Return of Love* in 1961. These novels are considered to be her major early work, in which she examines the human condition through everyday events such as jumble sales and walks in the woods. Her characters are unassuming people leading unremarkable lives; Pym was the chronicler of quiet lives.

In 1963, *An Unsuitable Attachment* was rejected by her publisher. In all, twenty publishers refused to publish this latest novel over the next few years. She was dismayed and a few years later her dismay was added to when she was diagnosed with breast cancer. In 1974 she suffered a minor stroke and retired from her work, devoting her time to a new novel about four office workers on the verge of retirement. This novel, *Quartet in Autumn*, was also rejected but then an extraordinary coincidence revived her fortunes.

In 1977 the *Times Literary Supplement* asked a number of leading writers and literary critics to name the writer they thought to be the century's most underrated novelist. The poet Philip Larkin and the critic Lord David Cecil both nominated Barbara Pym. With astonishing speed, she emerged from what she had termed "the wilderness" after sixteen years of obscurity to fame and fortune. *Quartet in Autumn* was accepted for publication in 1977 and it was short-listed for the Booker Prize. In 1978, *The Sweet Dove Died* was published and her new publishers Macmillan reprinted all her novels. Simultaneously they were published in America to huge acclaim and translated into many foreign languages. Pym began to enjoy international acclaim.

Sadly, a mere two years after her rediscovery, her cancer returned and this time, treatments were unsuccessful. She rushed to finish her new novel, *A Few Green Leaves*, and died at a hospice in Oxford in 1980.

Barbara Pym still has a big following, particularly in America where you can attend the annual conference of the Barbara Pym Society and listen to learned discussion of the "Men in Barbara Pym's Life" or "Class Differences in Barbara Pym's England". You can also purchase 'Cat' notecards, 'Aga' Christmas cards, or Barbara Pym Society mugs in green or pale blue. Tempting, eh?

So what is her work like?

David Cecil called her novels "unpretentious, subtle, accomplished...the finest examples of high comedy to have appeared in England in the past 75 years". Strong words, eh? And was he right? Judge for yourself from this not untypical example drawn from *The Sweet Dove Died:*

He is going to kiss me, Leonora thought in sudden panic, pray heaven no more than that. She tried to protest, even to scream, but no sound came. Humphrey was larger and stronger than she was and his kiss very different from the reverent touch on lips, cheek or brow which was all James seemed to want. One couldn't lose one's dignity, of course, Leonora told herself, for after all one wasn't exactly a young girl. Surely freedom from this sort of thing was among the compensations of advancing

*age and the sad decay of one's beauty; one really ought not
to have to fend people off any more.*

It's that killer "one", isn't it? And the constrained emotions encompassed within it and within the Leonora who thinks of herself thus. So different from the outward portrayals of sexual display and congress that are so much more typical of our period. And that, of course, is the fascination of Barbara Pym's writing, it seems to me. I shall read more. Will you?

As you leave Oswestry to the north you come upon the Old Oswestry Hillfort, first occupied probably by the tribe that was known as the Cornovii. This is an elaborate series of ditches and ramparts encircling a central plateau. Now we don't know much about the people who built and inhabited these Iron Age fortresses, although modern archaeological excavations reveal something about their way of life. The people almost certainly lived in roundhouses made with the branches of trees roughly interwoven and covered with mud or clay. An opening at the side served as a door and window and an uncovered point in the roof acted as a chimney. A fire in the middle would be used for cooking and for heating but the bare earth was the ground they ate off and slept on, covered only by animal skins.

However, this particular fortress has an association, in legend at least, which is of special interest. According to this legend, the fort was built by a giant named Ogyrfan, who lived at the same time as the famous King Arthur of the celebrated Round Table. Ogyrfan was the father of Guinevere, Arthur's wife, about whom it was said:

*"Guinevere, Giant Ogyrfan's daughter,
Naughty young, more naughty later."*

Now we all remember what happened to Guinevere, don't we? She betrayed Arthur by having it off with his faithful knight Lancelot and thus brought about the downfall of Camelot and the end of the Round Table. She was the earliest scarlet woman of English literature and her legendary image has come down through the centuries to us, even though the truth of its original is extremely difficult to fathom.

A French chronicler gives us another story about Old Oswestry concerning a stay here by William the Conqueror, whose warrior Pain Peverel:

> *"Proud and courageous Knight, cousin of the King, with his shield shining with gold, on which was a cross of azure indented, took fifteen knights with him, in the midst of a tempest of thunder and lightning, and fought and completely routed the fiend, who carried a club and was guarding a treasure of oxen, cows, swans, peacocks, horses and other animals made of fine gold, and there was a golden bull which told the events which were to come."*

On the western edge of Old Oswestry is the outline of Wat's Dyke and now you'll want to know who or what was Wat. The trouble is we do not know. There is no record of any person with such a name in Anglo-Saxon times, when it is believed this fortification was built. Even worse, for all you seekers after the truth, we know even less about the origins of Wat's Dyke than we do of Offa's Dyke. As far as we can tell, (Who?)Wat built his dyke between Basingwerk on the Dee estuary and south of Oswestry some time before Offa began his. Did Offa steal the idea from (Who?)Wat? Did Wat's Dyke serve as the northern end of Offa's fortification? Were they both designed to keep out the Taffs? The latter is the only question that can be answered with some confidence, since keeping out the Welsh has been a national sport of the English since time immemorial, as I have pointed out earlier.

Old Oswestry Hillfort and its surroundings is the site of legends. Still, I quite like to think of Guinevere strolling through the quiet pages of a Barbara Pym novel perhaps or maybe trying to work out what on earth Spooner could have meant when he hailed her thus:

"Here's a health to the queer old dean!"

15 Oswestry to Llangollen

Next morning I was up and away quite early, rejoining the Offa's Dyke Path at Oswestry Racecourse where an unusual piece of statuary of two horses' heads and a saddle commemorates the racing that used to take place on the circuit there. There's also a toposcope identifying the hills and mountains visible from its viewpoint. On that bright and breezy morning I could clearly pick out to the south the Clee Hills some thirty-five miles away, the Long Mynd and Stiperstones some twenty-five miles away, Breidden Hill and the Long Mountain closer to hand, and Plynlimon and Cader Idris some thirty-five miles to the west. Then it was back on the line of the actual Dyke, where it marches across fields and through woods, until you find yourself actually walking again on the top of the dyke. It's still impressive, it still inspires awe, and it is about to disappear. There are remnants of it some miles further north but these are largely on the industrial outskirts of Wrexham, where it does finally peter out, but the Path designers wisely decided to follow a different route for the final stages of the walk.

So, coming down the Ceiriog valley towards Chirk Castle which peeps out of the trees on the hillside above, I was reaching the end of my acquaintance with Offa's Dyke, as I entered the castle grounds and climbed on the nettle-strewn summertime permissive path up to the castle itself.

Chirk Castle was not, like so many castles in the Marches, built immediately after the Norman Conquest. Its construction was begun some 700 years ago, probably by one of the most powerful Marcher lords, Roger Mortimer (yes, one of that lot), as a reward for his support of the king against the Welsh, so its purpose was identical to its earlier counterparts, viz. to keep the boyos at bay.

It was originally not much more than a dungeon within a series of circular defensive towers, some of which contained 'murder holes'. Through these soldiers could pour boiling oil, or boiling urine, or any other unpleasant substance for that matter, on to any Taffies trying to batter the doors down below them.

The castle was added to over the next few centuries, as different Norman lords inhabited it, until Sir Thomas Myddleton finally purchased it in 1595 for £5,000 - a snip at half the price. Myddleton was a seriously rich man, who had been a founder of the East India Company that stole the wealth of India and made its native population into paupers, and an investor in the expeditions of Francis Drake (the bowler) and Walter Raleigh (the tobacconist). He spent lavishly to turn Chirk Castle into a comfortable Tudor residence. Myddleton was Lord Mayor of London in 1613 but it was his younger brother Hugh who was responsible for one of the most imaginative acts of his time. In order to provide fresh water to the ever-growing city of London, he organised the construction of a canal to carry fresh water to London from the Hertfordshire springs of Chadwell and Amwell, a distance of nearly 40 miles. This engineering feat, begun in 1609 and finished in 1613 (when it was officially declared open by his brother, the Lord Mayor), was so bold and thorough in design, that the "New River" source, as it came to be called, is still used today forming a valuable part of London's water supply. And all this was done while Sir Hugh Myddleton was promoting the uses of tobacco by appearing in public with his pal Sir Walter Raleigh, puffing away on a Capstan full-strength.

Sir Thomas's son, also Sir Thomas, became MP for Denbighshire in 1625 and thus found himself on Cromwell's side in the Civil Wars, becoming Sergeant Major General of the Parliamentary forces in North Wales. Trouble was, he was so busy duffing up the opposition elsewhere that he failed to protect his own home and Chirk was captured by the Royalists in 1643. After a bit of non-too-subtle bribery, the castle was regained and the general's son, Sir Thomas III, installed as governor, while his father changed sides. Mistake number two, for the Parliamentarians besieged Chirk and captured it in 1659, burning and demolishing large parts of it. When the Restoration came a year later, the Myddletons had some serious work to do to repair it. But they did, helped by a generous grant of £60,000 from the grateful Charles II.

Old wealth tends to hang around quite a while, as we all know, and the Myddleton family have lived in Chirk Castle ever since, doing a deal with the National Trust in 1978 so that it is maintained and open to public gazing, while they still live in one wing. The glossy about Chirk tells you all this as if there is something wonderful about a family who have managed to live in this manorial pile for centuries. Just remember, however, if you choose to spend some of your hard-earned visiting the place, how that wealth was accumulated and how much of the public purse has been raided over the centuries to maintain them in their Fancy Dan way of life.

The Dyke actually goes right through the grounds of Chirk Castle but the Path veers off slightly to the west, taking you along quiet roads and across fields till you reach the busy A5 road. On the other side of that, as you head down towards the Llangollen Canal is a short but distinct stretch of the Dyke that you walk alongside. And then, as the canal comes into view, it is gone. So with a final shout of "Bugger Offa!" at some recalcitrant Welsh cows that were gazing at me as if they had never seen an English person before, I bade my farewell to the actual Offa's Dyke and joined the towpath for the pleasant stroll to Froncysyllte and one of the wonders of its, and our, age.

Froncysyllte Aqueduct consists of nineteen spans of 126 feet above the River Dee and has an overall length of 1,007 feet. The tapering piers are solid for their first seventy feet and hollow for the remaining fifty feet. This not only saved on masonry and overall weight but also ensured a stable low centre of gravity for the structure. The trough is designed with the towpath supported on iron pillars over part of the waterway. The whole thing was built by the 36-year-old Thomas "Wee Tommy" Telford, the son of a Scottish shepherd who had just been appointed Surveyor of

Public Works for Shropshire and was to become one of the greatest civil engineers of his time. In its day Froncysyllte Aqueduct was revolutionary because aqueducts up to that time had been built with stone and Telford was at the forefront of using the new iron-making technology in innovative ways.

The whole thing took twelve years to construct but, when it finally opened on 26th November 1805, a huge crowd of spectators cheered the highly decorated narrowboats that crossed from Froncysyllte to the northern bank where the Telford Inn now stands. This was one month after the Battle of Trafalgar, remember, and patriotic feelings were running high. Consequently, it was no surprise to find a military band in one of the boats playing *God Save the King*.

It's still a remarkable piece of engineering and I have to admit I found it just a little scary to look over the edge down those 126 feet to the River Dee roaring below me as I took the narrow towpath alongside the canal trough and across to the opposite side of the gorge. I wasn't worried so much about myself as about some of those whom I met on the crossing - children who insisted on running and an elderly couple who kept stopping and turning round to see where they had come from. Passing such as these on that narrow strip of path required a certain amount of care and I was glad to reach the other side, where, conveniently, there was the Telford Inn inviting me to take my lunch.

If I tell you that the Telford Inn boasts that it has a function room, I think you'll understand that it is not really suited to solitary walkers like me but rather to coach parties of old dears from Runcorn or Rochdale. Notices abound about what you can and can't do in its grounds, amongst which was one forbidding the eating of anything other than that purchased on the premises. But, hey! the sun was shining and I thought that at least the beer would be good.

It wasn't, actually. Tetley's bitter rarely is especially good, but I drank it anyway then slunk off down under the aqueduct to eat my stowed-away sandwiches, near a couple of Welsh scallies wearing Burberry baseball caps to proclaim their wannabe-hooligan status.

Then it was back into climbing mode, as I followed the Path on its attractive way up through Trevor Wood and on to the narrow road known as the Panorama Walk. This has been famous for at least two centuries, when it would have been walked by those who visited the picturesque Llangollen. Did Wordsworth tread this way? Did Walter Scott? It is not impossible, for both came to visit the Ladies of Llangollen whom you will be pleased to meet shortly. I guess the Panorama Walk was originally a miners' track for the hills around here have been extensively quarried and mined over the centuries. It certainly provides exquisite views of the Dee valley below and the town of Llangollen that was to provide my lodging that night and of the scree slopes of the hills behind.

Before I descended to Llangollen, however, I climbed up to the remains of the Castell Dinas Bran hill fort. It's a steep climb but well waymarked and worth it for the stupendous views from the top. This was originally an Iron Age fort and local legend has it that it houses the Holy Grail of Arthurian legend, though we're all still looking for that, aren't we?

People from Llangollen used to greet the arrival of the sun's rays on Easter Sunday on the top of Dinas Bran by dancing three somersaults, although nowadays they make do with a pilgrimage to the top of the mountain. In other areas, a basin of water was taken to the top of the nearest hill to catch the reflection of the sun dancing on the horizon. Odd or what?

The hill may have been the site of a castle built by Eliseg, Prince of Powys in the sixth century, but it was definitely colonised in the thirteenth century by Gruffud ap Madog who built his castle here. However, it appears it was only occupied for a short period at a time when war between the Norman Marcher lords and the Welsh was at its fiercest. Somewhere near the end of that century it was sacked and burned. It was not a suitable place for a civil settlement and so those that remained moved to the bottom of the hill to found Llangollen.

I followed in their footsteps.

The entry to Llangollen from the hillside takes you across the stone bridge over the River Dee, which hurtles over rocks with foamy rapids below you. It is easy to see why this was once a place to visit on the Grand Tour of Picturesque Sights in the nineteenth century. Unfortunately, it's been all downhill since then as hordes of tourists have followed their more discerning forebears to take nostalgic trips on the Llangollen Railway Society's steam trains or on horse-drawn barges along the canal. Those latter-day tourists are catered for by shops that sell chips, Welsh flags, sticks of rock, candyfloss and all the other rubbish that someone has decided are essential items for visitors to select as mementoes of their stay. Epitomising the downfall of Llangollen is the Royal Hotel on the opposite side of the bridge and overlooking the river. This, which must once have been the major hotel in the town, is in a sad state of disrepair and is a poor advert for the town.

Cambrian House where I was staying is a much pleasanter place. It is run by Roger Honey, a friendly and outgoing character, who showed me to my room and explained procedures. I was a little taken aback to find that my bed was already occupied by a teddy bear and, when I went to the bathroom I found there were teddy bears everywhere - at the top of the stairs, outside my room, in the loo. It looked like they'd taken over. As I left the building to go in search of something to eat, I bumped into Roger and asked him what it was all about.

"They're the reason I'm here," he explained. "I inherited six when my mother died and at the time I was looking for a change of career. When we came here, it just seemed the right thing to do to use the bears around the place."

"But there must be more than six bears," I said.

"Since we've been here, the six have grown to fifty-three," he answered. "Only one has 'walked' in all that time. People are very honest really. There's a Teddy Bear Fair in town in June every year and people who come to it just love to stay here."

"I bet they do," I said, wondering what sort of sad people they were. I've had a go before now about this phenomenal growth in the number of teddy bears in Britain (and, for all I know, the world) and I'm beginning to think it's about time I formed a society to free the world from teddy bears. I could sell 'Teddy Bear Free Zone' posters to guesthouses and hotels. Our theme song could be the *Teddy Bears' Funeral*, to the tune of the *Teddy Bears' Picnic*.

Still, each to his own. I picked up a leaflet as I left. It was advertising another speciality of Cambrian House - its Body and Soul Centre, which shares the premises. It offers reflexology ("a wonderful relaxing foot massage, each point on the foot reflecting different glands and organs in the body"), Indian head massage ("creates a feeling of Peace and Calm"), together with more common feminine beauty treatments like manicures, pedicures, eyebrow tinting, bikini waxing, and deep cleanse facials.

I was tempted but decided to head for the CAMRA-recommended Sun Inn instead. The landlord there, a tall bloke with long ponytail and beard and wearing sandals, was explaining to one of his customers how he used to fetch barrels of beer himself from obscure breweries on a trailer attached to the back of his car, until someone nicked his trailer. Nowadays, he gets his beer delivered and I have to say he had a splendid range on display that evening. I tried several of them, purely in the interests of research of course, and they were so good that my brain went into some kind of senior moment so that I had no recollection of the two hours I'd been there when I did eventually stagger back to Cambrian House. I do recall, however, that my decision to leave arose from my realisation that at about nine o'clock there were only four other people in the bar - and none of us were speaking. There was a fat bloke sat on a tall stool at the bar; there were two old caps sat also sat at the bar; and there was a middle-aged bloke reading the paper at a table. The only sound was some solid rhythm n' blues belting out from the jukebox.

I had noted a TV programme that I thought I might enjoy about Rod Hull, who had a dummy called Emu that was little more than an extension to his right arm but with which he wreaked havoc wherever he appeared. His most famous occasion, still so fondly remembered that it was recently voted number 13 in TV's Greatest Moments, was when he pulled interviewer Michael Parkinson down to the ground, so much to the annoyance of the silver-haired Parky that he still never talks about it. When I got back to my room, I switched on the TV and tried to find the programme. But it was on Channel 4 and I was in Wales and what you get in Wales is TeleWele. So I couldn't watch Rod and Emu.

With an oath of "Bugger Offa!", I went to bed instead.

16 Llangollen

"Exterminate! Exterminate!"

No, that's not the most obvious sound you'd expect to hear in Llangollen, is it? You were probably expecting something like the glorious racket of a Welsh valleys male voice choir or maybe an oratorio sung by some Italian tenor. And you will hear all those sounds at the magnificent Llangollen International Eisteddfod, held every summer in the Royal Pavilion, when thousands descend on the town to witness the proceedings.

Now, we'll come to the Eisteddfod later. But I want to return to the opening words of this section, for those unforgettable imperatives, spoken through a vibrating microphone, were the call sign of the Daleks, Doctor Who's greatest enemies. And the *Doctor Who Experience* is situated right here in the middle of Llangollen. Who? you might be asking, if you are not old enough to remember the TV cavortings of the United Kingdom's favourite children's sci-fi series, played out over thirty plus years. So, for the record and to refresh those of ancient brain, I'd better just give you a brief run down.

Doctor Who began life on BBC television in November 1963. It originated as a kids' TV programme to fill the gap between *Grandstand* and *Juke Box Jury*. Its main premise was of a strange character, called The Doctor (nobody ever asked him "Doctor Who?" or what he was a doctor of), who was able to travel through time. That first episode saw The Doctor, played by William Hartnell, travelling back in his Tardis, which was really an old blue police box, into Earth's past to help some rather slow-witted cavemen to discover fire. But it was with the second episode that the series really took off. For that episode featured the scary Daleks, whose war-cry was "Exterminate!" and who looked to have been made with egg-boxes glued together on to a large traffic cone. Not to Mary Whitehouse they didn't! For the president of the National Viewers and Listeners Association, the self-appointed guardian of the nation's morals, fell hook line and sinker for the rather amateur animation of these monsters from outer space and tried to get it taken off air, calling the programme "teatime brutality for tots".

I suspect her complaints served to make the programme even more popular and by the time a whole series was devoted to *The Genesis of the Daleks*, nine and a half million people were watching as the distinctive *Oooo-Eeeee-Oooooow* theme music, created on one of the first synthesisers at the BBC Radiophonic Workshop, whistled through the evening air. The Doctor was anywhere between 750 and 953 years old at various stages of his journeys and, thanks to the cleverness of the original concept (and a lot of suspended disbelief on the part of his viewers) was able to transmogrify periodically into a different actor in different, though equally eccentric, clothes. Thus William Hartnell was followed in turn by Patrick Troughton, Jon Pertwee, Tom Baker, Peter Davison, Colin Baker (no relation), and Sylvester McCoy, until the BBC pulled the plug on his Tardis in 1989.

That merely served to ensure his immortality in the minds of his fans world-wide, who refer to themselves - though not in public for fear of being exterminated by you know who - as Whovians. There are, literally, hundreds of fan clubs throughout the world - in New Zealand, Australia, Canada, Norway, Germany, Luxembourg, and the USA, as well as Britain. Some of them have adopted appropriate names like The Time Meddlers of Los Angeles or the Thames Valley Time Lords but I rather like the sound of The Society of the Rusting Tardis in Washington and the Who-Ligans in Cornwall. You can also attend the annual Whovention in Sydney, the annual Gallifrey One Convention in Los Angeles, or the Destiny Convention in Northampton. If you're really keen, you can sign up for the Doctor Who 40th Anniversary Cruise but you'll have to be quick (not to mention half-crazy)!

At the doorway to the *Doctor Who Experience*, you are met by a replica Dalek named Norman, that is completely silent, immobile and unthreatening, and you do rather wonder how it managed to get up the steps to its position. Inside, after paying rather a lot of money, you are confronted by a Tardis and then taken through some gloomy corridors with lights flashing intermittently, where you see a variety of costumes worn by the various Doctors, and past a mock-up of the Tardis console (where a notice apologises that you cannot touch it because it was vandalised within 30 minutes of being placed there! - send the Daleks after them, I say). Then you are guided into a room called the Hall of Monsters where more flashing lights pop on and off as you gaze tremulously at the rather cheaply-made models used to scare the living daylights out of us all. Remember The Kandyman? The Garm? The Cybermen? The Gastropod? The Silurians?

It was just too much. I was glad to get back into the daylight and visit the giftshop, where I couldn't decide between a Cyberman Bottlestopper and a set of tasteful Doctor Who coasters, but in the end bought neither. Then I discovered why this exhibition is housed here in Llangollen. It's all to do with the fact that the Dapol factory, which makes toys and is housed in this building, used to make the bases for the Daleks. In truth, the exhibition is rather naff, but that's the whole point of it really. All those Whovians and their fan clubs are indulging in a little post-modern irony, aren't they?

Personally, I'm with the Daleks. Let's save the human race from Whovians now.

"Exterminate! Exterminate!"

There is a sign in the garden of Plas Newydd which reads NO BALL GAMES. This has to be the most ironic sign ever planted, for Plas Newydd was the home of the legendary "two most celebrated virgins in Europe". These were the Ladies of Llangollen, Sarah Ponsonby and Eleanor Butler, who have been subsequently claimed by what Julie Burchill calls the Muffia as exemplary early lesbians. And I will desist from comments about Offa's Dykes, so don't even think about that. So, who were they and what were they doing in Llangollen? It's an intriguing tale.

Eleanor Butler and Sarah Ponsonby were members of the Anglo-Irish aristocracy, the former aged thirty-four and the latter aged eighteen, who in 1780 shocked contemporary society by eloping from Ireland against the wishes of their families. Accompanied by their faithful maid, Mary "Molly the Bruiser" Caryll, they sailed to Holyhead and embarked on a tour of Wales, settling in the Vale of Llangollen and purchasing Plas Newydd on a hill just outside the town but with views of Castell Dinas Bran. There, over the next fifty years, they lived a life "of sweet and delicious retirement", which in those days - hey! in all days, if you're lucky enough to get it - was the cool thing to do. What did this retirement entail? Well, in their case they wrote, read, sketched and embroidered and transformed their house and gardens.

The house is a sort of fairy-tale dwelling. It has the typically English black and white theme on the outside, rather overdone so it looks like a set of large magpies have taken root there. But once you get closer, you see how eccentric it really is. Outside there are carvings of fantastic animals or of nude figures over doors and heraldic stained glass windows. Inside there's a four-poster bed with velvety drapes and cushions, leatherwork, carved oak panelling, polished faces, and mysterious hallways.

It wasn't just the house that was eccentric. The Ladies of Llangollen were noted for their unusual dress sense:

Miss Butler is tall and masculine, she wears always a riding habit, hangs her hat with the air of a sportsman in the hall, and appears in all respects as a young man, if we except the petticoats which she still retains. Miss Ponsonby, on the contrary, is polite and effeminate, fair and beautiful.

That was from a rather bitchy (sorry!) account in a newspaper of the day. Although they were upset by what they perceived as the insinuations of this piece, the Ladies became celebrities and were feted in Llangollen. They were in attendance at the opening of Telford's splendid Froncysyllte Aqueduct in 1804. They were visited by some noteworthy contemporaries. The Duke of Wellington, Sir Walter Scott, and Josiah Wedgwood all called for a cup of tea. And William Wordsworth and Robert Southey both composed rather crappy poems while staying there.

But it's the fascination about their love lives that really keeps them commemorated. They referred to their relationship as "romantic friendship" but some of their female visitors were less complimentary. "Damned sapphists" was how one described them while another was reluctant "to pronounce such attachments uncemented by something more tender still than friendship". And some have claimed there is a coded message in this statement from Eleanor Butler's diary:

"My beloved and I spent a delightful evening in the shrubbery"

Strong stuff, eh?

Certainly the Lesbian Gay Bisexual Transgender Resource Center of California has no doubts about the Ladies' sexuality nor does Llinell Lesbiaid Gogledd Cymru. Both organisations proudly claim them for their own. Indeed the former has recently acquired two lovely African pygmy frogs named Eleanor and Sarah after the Llangollen twosome, while the latter lists them among several other noted lesbians who have settled in North Wales.

Me? I'm with the Muffia. I'd love to have met these two remarkable ladies who defied convention and yet became accepted in this small town in mid-Wales because of who they were, not because of their particular sexual proclivities.

Sisters are Doing it for Themselves sang Annie Lennox about the liberated 1980s. It could as easily have applied to the liberated Ladies of Llangollen in the 1780s.

I have written elsewhere about the comparatively modern origins of the eisteddfod but the Llangollen International Eisteddfod has a quite different derivation, being the brainchild of a Liverpool journalist called Harold Tudor, a music publisher called Gwynn Williams and a grammar school teacher called George Northing. These three men launched their idea to the unsuspecting townsfolk of Llangollen in the spring of 1946, persuaded large numbers of them to get involved in various ways, and devised a series of musical competitions for choirs and individuals. Helped by the British Council, they distributed details of these competitions throughout war-ravaged Europe, and then set about the mammoth task of finding accommodation, organising hospitality, hiring equipment *et cetera*. Then they waited for the arrival of what they hoped would be the first international competitors in June 1947.

Would they come? How would they get there? The various committees, together with Harold Tudor, Gwynn Williams and George Northing, bit their nails and prayed. But they did arrive - some sang their way across Europe to pay for their journey, others hitchhiked, others hired their own coaches. The first to get there was a Portuguese choir whose coach was cheered through Llangollen's narrow streets. They were followed by others, including the Madrigalisti Citta di Milano and the Hungarian Workers Choir.

That was the start of it all and the Eisteddfod has grown in strength and fame since those early days. One of the most remembered choirs was the Obernkirchen Children's Choir from Germany, whom Dylan Thomas described as "pigtailed angels", with their rendering in the 1953 children's choir competition of a little-known German folksong *The Happy Wanderer*, which went on to become an international hit record. This song has a particular resonance for me since it became the unofficial anthem of my football team, Wolverhampton Wanderers. Ah, those innocent days when we used to sing:

Up the Wolves, up the Wolves, up the Wolves
Up the W - O - L - V - E - S, the Wolves
Up the Wolves
The team in gold and black

Well! It's much nicer than "You're a bastard referee", isn't it?

Since 1947, countless members of the great and the good have appeared at Llangollen. Conductors like Sir John Barbiroli and Sir Adrian Boult, opera singers like Joan Sutherland, Placido

Domingo, Luciano Pavarotti, Bryn Terfel, musicians like James Galway, Julian Lloyd Webber, Igor Oistrakh and Yehudi Menuhin have all graced the stage there.

There's an amusing story told about Placido Domingo's appearance there in 1968. Waiting back stage to go on, he was anxious to loosen his vocal chords by doing a few tra-la-las but was unable to do so for fear of disturbing the onstage proceedings. The problem was overcome by a lady from the committee peeping through the curtains and, when the applause broke out, signalling to the Italian tenor, who went through his vocal exercises until a second signal told him to clam up.

Nowadays something like 2,500 competitors from 40 different countries participate and over 100,000 people attend during the six days of competition to bear witness to this remarkable dream of three men at the end of the hostilities that tore Europe apart in the middle of the twentieth century.

It is truly extraordinary.

My old friend George Borrow, author of *Wild Wales*, spent quite some time in Llangollen in the mid-1800s, making it his headquarters for much of his time in north Wales and parking his wife and daughter there for the duration of his expeditions. He mentions Plas Newydd, which he visited, but not the *Doctor Who Experience*, though I'm sure he would have taken pleasure therein. He also writes at length about St Collen, after whom the town is named, though to tell the truth it's all a typical Borrovian embellishment of an old Welsh legend and of little interest.

One place he did visit and write about is located a mile or so northwards out of Llangollen, in a secluded and beautiful valley. Nowadays there is a very large caravan and camping site situated there. It is very ugly and a real blot on the landscape. The site has been there for a long time and will probably still be there when the Martians land to take over the planet (or will it be the Daleks?).

What is so especially dispiriting about it is that this plethora of portakabins, this cornucopia of caravans, this extravaganza of

Elsans, is placed right next to the ruins of the beautiful Valle Crucis Abbey and within a stone's throw of the remarkable Pillar of Eliseg. Valle Crucis was a Cistercian Abbey, built in 1201 by the then Prince of Powys. It had a turbulent history, being ravaged by fire shortly after it had been built, severely damaged again by Edward I in his wars against Llewellyn ap Gruffud, and then later in the time of Owen Glendower, before finally being made redundant in 1538 by Henry VIII's dissolution of the monasteries. But it is, or rather its remaining shell is, a beautiful building.

While visiting Valle Crucis, Borrow encountered a woman in part of the ruin that had come to be used as a farmhouse. He asked her if she knew where Iolo Goch was buried. The woman confessed that she had never heard of this name, which gave old George the opportunity to bore the pants off her with his learning. Iolo Goch, he explained, was Owen Glendower's court bard and "assisted his cause wonderfully by the fiery odes, in which he incited the Welsh to rise against the English". Nobody on the site at the time knew about Iolo Goch's burial place, except George Borrow, and I haven't been able to find any modern information about this either. So it looks like another product of Borrow's fertile mind.

He also visited the nearby Pillar of Eliseg, which is the remaining phallic shaft of a cross standing about seven feet high on a mound in the middle of a field. Borrow, being the cleverclogs that he was, told his guide that the stone should properly be known as "Colofn Eliseg, in Saxon the Ellisian column". What he didn't know was that the stone was actually erected in the first half of the 9th century by Concenn the great-grandson of Eliseg "who annexed the inheritance of Powys through the nine years from the power of the English which he made into a sword-land by fire. Whosoever shall read this hand-inscribed stone, let him give a blessing on the soul of Eliseg". This is the barely-visible legend on the stone itself.

One thing he did get right, however, was his description of the monks' fishpond, situated behind the roofless abbey. This is the oldest surviving fishpond in Wales, having existed for eight hundred years. The monks would have sat there every Friday morning to catch some carp to accompany their chips and mushy peas. And rumour has it that, to this day, there is a giant carp at the bottom of the pond which has been there for over two hundred years. Its name is Dallyth and that is where the creators of *Doctor Who* got the name for their little exterminators!

Really! Ask George Borrow, if you don't believe me.

17 Llangollen to Ruthin

I returned to the Panorama Walk above Llangollen the next morning, following the road for the first mile or so until the Offa's Dyke Path takes you off on to a track across the scree slopes of Eglwyseg Mountain. Here a notice asks climbers to avoid rock-climbing between March and July because of the nesting activities of a protected species of birds. The walk across the scree is tremendous, though I could imagine in bad weather when the mist is down it's probably a bit scary. As I was approaching below the sheer cliff face of Craig Arthur, a great screeching began up in the rocks that continued as I walked. I guessed that this must be one of the birds mentioned in the warning notice and I also worked out that the screeching was probably intended to keep me at a distance. I was curious, however, as to what this bird was and so, though I probably shouldn't have, I clapped my hands and shouted "Bugger Offa!" to see what would happen.

A huge bird flew out of a cleft in the rock face and wheeled overhead, still emitting its warning shriek. It was clearly a peregrine falcon and, since the only thing that was moving within a hundred yards of it was yours truly, I was pretty sure that the shrieks were definitely aimed at me. It was obviously protecting its young, who would have been in the nest in the cliff. Peregrine falcons in flight are one of the finest sights in the world, as they swoop from the heavens at incredible speeds but they are also one of the most persecuted birds in Britain. There are still sadly people who seek to steal peregrine falcon eggs, risking a prison sentence. I hope they end up sharing a cell with Dr Harold Shipman, the Cheshire mass murderer.

As you leave the cliff face behind you, the Path descends through forestation to a bleak spot known as World's End where it rejoins the road and follows it up on to the even bleaker moor which is crossed by a boardwalk. The Llandegla Forest entered at the end of this boardwalk has a notice that announces it belongs to the Shotton Mill Paper Company, Britain's largest manufacturer of newsprint. As I walked through the pleasant pine-needled forest paths, accompanied by the sound of chainsaws somewhere else in the forest, I wondered whether the copy of *The Guardian* I had bought in Llangollen that morning originated here in Llandegla Forest. Well, there was a large article about Tiger Woods in it!

By lunchtime I had emerged from the forest and was approaching the village of Llandegla itself when, as I climbed over a stile, I saw a notice inviting me to visit The Crown pub a couple of hundred yards off the Path. Now you know me, the invitation was too good to refuse and so off I toddled.

The landlord who served me explained that he had only been there less than a year and that the pub wasn't referenced in the Offa's Dyke Association literature because the previous landlord used to stay shut at lunchtimes from Sunday to Wednesday, whereas he intended to be open regularly.

"What bitter do you recommend?" I asked, for a large sign stated that this was a J.W. Lees pub and I had never heard of this brewery.

"The Scorcher's very nice," he said. "It's the brewery's summer special. Nice and light and hoppy."

Ever willing to test new hop products in the interests of research, I ordered a pint and indeed it was as he had described.

"Who is J.W. Lees?" I asked, after my long first draught had slaked my thirst. "Never heard of him."

"It's a Manchester brewery."

"Manchester? What they doing here in Wales?"

"They've got a chain of pubs in North Wales," he explained, passing me a postcard that showed the location of each pub in this chain that stretched from Wrexham to Holyhead.

I noticed a poster on the wall of the bar that proclaimed 'A pint of John Willie's does you good', or something to that effect.

"Does it really market itself as John Willie's?" I asked, laughing in amazement.

"Oh yes," the landlord replied, also grinning. "Even the ladies like John Willie's."

He should have been in marketing, not running a pub. His wicked suggestion reminded me of the advert for Irn-bru I had seen on that bus back near Pandy. Don't we just love our *double entendres?*

Two pints of John Willie's Scorcher made me very mellow and I set out in the afternoon sunlight feeling very confident that the next section's walking was comfortably within my grasp and I could take my time. So, I duly passed through Llandegla village and took the signposted track between the church of St Teclas and the Old Rectory. St Thecla, after whom the church is named, was a woman who heard St Paul preaching about virginity and was so impressed that she broke off her engagement and spent her life promoting virginity. So she wouldn't have tasted John Willie's Scorcher, would she?

There was a well dedicated to St Teclas in the village and there's a curious old legend attached to this well, concerning a farmer called Robert Wiliam, his wife Mari and their only child Wiliam who was subject to fits. When the boy was twelve, his parents became especially anxious about him because so many omens of death occurred. Apple trees burst into blossom too soon; an old cock (John Willie again) started crowing in the middle of the night; Robert Wiliam met an old hag who vanished after muttering some frightening words; and then he met a corpse candle moving along the road ahead of him one night.

So, scared out of his wits, Robert Wiliam went to see the local wise man and was told what to do. He took his son to the church and left him by the well, with a cock in a basket. Young Wiliam had to walk around the well three times repeating the Lord's Prayer, then do the same around the church, before sleeping that night inside. In the morning he placed sixpence on the altar, left the cock beside it and went home. A week later a messenger came to the family home to say that the cock had died and that the disease, which had been transferred to it, had died also.

Young Wiliam completely recovered from his illness and went on to reach a ripe old age. During his life, he impregnated as many young virgins as he could, with shouts of 'John Willie's does you good'.

Actually I made the last bit up but the rest is a proper cock and bull story, isn't it? (Okay, minus the bull).

Shortly after leaving the village, I crossed a footbridge where I met a dishevelled clutch of teenagers, all weighed down with heavy packs and looking really knackered.

"Are we anywhere near the village?" one of the girls called out to me.

"Do you mean Llandegla?" I asked, using my best Welsh pronunciation.

"Yes, I think that's the place. How far is it?" she asked again.

"You're virtually there," I replied, pointing back behind me, subtly demonstrating my superior navigational skills. "Just across those fields and you'll be in it. The path is clearly marked."

"The Offa's Dyke Path?" one of the boys quizzed.

"Yes, are you walking it too?"

"A bit of it," another boy replied. "We're doing our Duke of Edinburgh. We've got to get to the campsite just the other side of the village."

"Well, you're virtually there," I said, confidently. "Good luck."

And I turned from them to proceed on my way.

Fifteen minutes later I reached a road, which was about fifteen minutes earlier than I was expecting to. And the road had a pronounced bend in it where my map indicated it should be straight. I turned left and in five minutes found myself beside St Teclas's church in Llandegla again. That would teach me to mock an ancient Welsh legend. That would teach me not to be so cocky (sorry!) about my map-reading skills that I could patronise youngsters. That would teach me the effects of drinking two pints of John Willie's Scorcher at lunchtime when I still had six miles to walk.

I felt very foolish as I passed between the church and the Old Rectory for the second time within half an hour. This time I was very careful with the waymarking and made sure that I only followed the signs with the acorn that indicate the Offa's Dyke Path and ignored any other signposting. And this time I made no mistake.

A bit further on my route I saw another group of youngsters huddled over a map at the opposite corner of a field to me. One of them came sprinting across to me.

"Excuse me," she said. "Can you show me where we are on my map? We think we're a bit lost."

I looked at her and thought about my own wayward map reading that had taken me on a circular tour of Llandegla.

"Are you heading for Llandegla?" I asked.

"Yes."

"Following Offa's Dyke?"

"Yes."

"Duke of Edinburgh expedition?"

"Yes."

"What is it? Gold? Silver?"

"No, only bronze. We're not that good. That's why we're lost."

"Look, I've been walking all my life and I've just gone round in a complete circle. Don't worry about it. We all make mistakes. The important thing is to recognise them and put them right."

By this time the rest of her group had joined us and I pointed out the way I had just come on the map, as well as telling them what to look out for on the way.

"But what about all those bulls by the stile?" the first girl asked, pointing at where I had just come from.

"They're only bullocks," I said, as if I was the world's leading expert on matters bovine. "They won't touch you. All you need to do is clap your hands and shout 'Bugger Offa!' and they'll move. You'll see."

As soon as I said it, I regretted it. I could see them filling in their diaries that evening and telling about this man who told them to swear at cattle and then their teacher reading those diaries some time later and thinking they'd bumped into some total nutter. But it was too late. John Willie had done for me again. I said goodbye and left them to try their luck with the bullocks.

The rest of the afternoon passed off uneventfully, thank God.

I was now embarking on the first hills in the Clwydian Range that were to be my companions virtually until I reached near the end of the walk at Prestatyn. The initial climbing was challenging enough, with one or two breathless bits but overall I made reasonable progress over the heather-clad hills with occasional views of the Vale of Clwyd to the west, including the town of Ruthin that I was to visit that night. As I descended the final slope towards the Clwyd Gate Motel, I was left speechless by the sudden sight of a red kite, the story of whose survival is one of the most remarkable examples of bird protection I have come across.

Many people consider the red kite to be the most beautiful bird of prey in Britain, if not in the whole of Europe, but by 1956 there were only eight known pairs of kites in existence in the United Kingdom, all nesting in mid-Wales. This bird, which in Elizabethan times had been a frequent scavenger of the meat dropped in the unhygienic streets of London, was persecuted over the centuries by gamekeepers and farmers because of the belief that it preyed on chickens, pheasants and lambs. Shooting, poisoning and trapping all took their toll of the kite population and then the extensive use of man-made chemicals such as DDT on the fields further decimated those that still remained. It was at this low point that the Royal Society for the Protection of Birds stepped in and began their rescue mission. It has taken time but now there are upwards of 200 breeding pairs of red kites in Britain, mostly in mid-Wales but increasingly being introduced to other parts of the island.

This kite, wheeling in the sunlight and flashing its chestnut-red body in flight, was one of this new and wider population. I watched it in awe for several minutes as it scoured the ground, occasionally dipping suddenly for a closer look, before it disappeared into the nearby woodland.

The pub I stayed in that night was just outside Ruthin and I had to arrange a lift into the town itself, after I had deposited my stuff in my room. When I returned in the early evening, I went to the bar to order food and enjoy a pint or two (or four actually) of Wells's Bombardier ale, while I read *The Guardian*.

The place was quite busy, this being a Friday evening with many people obviously beginning their weekend in hope that the current sunshine would continue. A couple of men of about my age were discussing the pleasures of their forthcoming retirements at a table next to mine; a younger couple with a child aged about seven or eight were talking in Welsh to each other; at the bar a group were chatting to the landlady who clearly knew them well as regular visitors.

Suddenly a new figure appeared - a small, skinny man with long grey hair and a long grey beard. He looked like something out of a Tolkien novel, a hobbit perhaps or something of that sort.

"Greetings," he called out as he entered, and he spread his right arm out in a theatrical gesture towards the landlady, though the volume of his voice suggested he was including everyone within hearing. "The wanderer returns."

"Hello, Ieuan," said the landlady as she pulled a pint. "Usual is it?"

"A pint of your finest nectar, if you would be so kind," his voice boomed around the room.

"Back for the eisteddfod?" she asked. "Have you got tickets?"

"Indeed I have," said Bilbo Baggins. "For the whole week. I would not miss it for the world. The flowering of Welsh culture."

She served him and he stood away from the bar, looking around the room for somewhere to sit and, I thought to myself, for someone to sit by and irritate. I looked quickly down at my newspaper.

"Forgive my enquiry," I heard him say a few minutes later, not to me but to a couple who had just been served with drinks after him, had ordered a meal in the restaurant, and had sat down. "I couldn't help overhearing your name. A proud Welsh name, if I may be so bold. You wouldn't perchance be related to *the* Hopkins?"

"Well, yes I am actually," the man replied in a much lower voice, clearly embarrassed at this interruption to his intended quiet Friday evening. "I'm a second cousin, though I don't talk about it much. We were never that close."

"Ah, what an actor," proclaimed Bilbo, waving his arms about now as if he was playing Hamlet. "I was on the stage once with him, you know. What a talent!"

The man looked at his female companion, who was clasping his hand tightly and stifling a laugh at this preposterous little man.

"Are you on the stage now?" the man asked.

"Alas, no!" said the Hobbit. "My thespian days are over. I fear I shall never tread the boards again, shall never smell the greasepaint, shall never more fret my hour thereon."

And he put his right hand to his brow in mock anguish.

I wanted to applaud but feared that in doing so I would be inviting him to join me at my table. So I looked down again at my newspaper.

"Are you from round here?" asked the man who claimed to be related to Anthony (or was it Mary?) Hopkins.

"My grandparents are buried in the churchyard out there," said Bilbo. "The Clwydian hills were the first thing I saw when I arose each morn as a child. This… " He paused for dramatic effect and placed his fisted hand against his left breast. "… is *my* country."

He was beginning to sound more and more like Dylan Thomas's Reverend Eli Jenkins in *Under Milk Wood*, but at that moment the couple he had been speaking to were called through to the restaurant and he had lost the front row of his audience. So he sat down and, out of the corner of my eye, I could see his frog-like eyes flashing around the bar in search of someone else to bore. I kept my head down and then I heard his deep booming voice addressing the young couple in Welsh. I looked up briefly to see their reaction, which at first was more of the 'Who d'you think you are, short-arse?' variety than welcoming. But then politeness took over and they tolerated his questioning and no doubt further claims of greatness thrust aside, until his own meal arrived.

"Ah, lamb from the slaughter," he laughed at his own feeble joke, no doubt recited for the thousandth time, as his plate was placed before him.

I had had enough. I left him to his food and went to bed.

18 Ruthin

From wherever you start walking in Ruthin, you end up climbing the hill to the rather-wonderful St Peter's Square, which was of course where the town originally grew and was the reason for its growth at the southerly end of the Vale of Clwyd. I have to qualify my praise for its architectural attractiveness because many of its oldest buildings are now occupied by the moneylenders. Yes, I mean the banks who buy up these wonderful old properties in the middle of too many towns, fill them with carpets and central heating, plonk a few expensively-uniformed women with large backsides behind glass partitions, and then wait for us mugs to give them more of our money to play with. And for this privilege they charge us exorbitant amounts of interest, provide barely-adequate service (why aren't they open on Saturdays, for instance?) and then use our money to buy some other imposing and historic building.

Anyway one of these banks, the National Westminster, was once the old courthouse and the beam that was used as a gibbet still projects from its northerly exterior wall. There are several cellars underneath where prisoners used to be kept; these are now used for keeping bank managers out of sight of their customers. On another of its walls there is a sign which states that this is the spot where Owen Glendower first raised his troops to rebel against the English throne and this is therefore an appropriate spot to recount the story.

Owain Glyn Dwr, to give him his Welsh spelling, was descended from the princes of Wales who by the time of his birth in 1349 had become fully absorbed into English society. As befitting his high birth he was brought up in noble households, as a ward to the Earl of Arundel, and then studied law at the Inns of Court in London for several years. This would have been contemporaneous with his military service, which was normal in those times, and he earned a high reputation in battle as a man of great courage and strength. On the death of his father, Owain inherited the family estate at Sycharth not far from Oswestry, where he married and produced a large family and where his favourite bard Iolo Goch composed poems in his honour.

And there they might all have lived happily ever after, if it hadn't been for Lord Grey of Ruthin, who was a typical medieval baron, exacting dues and taxing traders and markets and generally making himself very unpopular with his Welsh subjects. Grey made the mistake, however, of picking a fight with his neighbour, Owain Glyn Dwr, which was not a very wise thing to do. For a start Owain was his social equal, secondly the Welsh had a long-standing grievance over the destruction of their self-governance by English kings of the past, and thirdly he was a better soldier than Grey was. The dispute began in 1400 over a piece of land on the border between each man's territory. Grey seized it and so Owain went to London to seek justice.

"I wish redress from Lord Grey who has illegally seized some of my land", Owain told the officials.

"And who, may I ask are you?" said one of the officials, Sir Cholmondley Jobsworth. "And why should we listen to your complaint?"

"I am Owain Glyn Dwr," came the answer, "and of some importance in my own country".

"And what country is this?" sneered Sir Cholmondley Jobsworth.

"A country of great pride, a country of poets, of musicians and brave fighters. The country of Wales."

"Oh that country!" Jobsworth sniggered. "I am sorry but in the circumstances, there is nothing we can do for you. We are not able to give you any sort of hearing. You yourself will have to settle your quarrel with Lord Grey."

So that's exactly what he did. He returned to Wales, gathered his army and marched to Ruthin, where they burned the town to the ground in the way they did in those days. And not content with that, with the smell of smoke well and truly up their noses, they went on and did the same to half the towns in North Wales. Suddenly all Wales was agog. Welsh scholars at Oxford and Cambridge downed their quills and headed home to write Press Releases and Welsh labourers living in England downed their shovels and armed themselves with bows and arrows. The uprising had begun. And this time the Taffs were gonna make those Anglo-Normans pay!

What is remarkable was that Glyn Dwr's rebellion lasted the best part of twelve years, despite the superior forces that the king, Henry IV (Parts 1 and 2), had at his command. In the course of this lengthy campaign he captured the odious Lord Grey, beat Edmund Mortimer at the Battle of Pilleth (whose site I had passed earlier in my trek), seized Cardiff, Aberystwyth and Harlech, held the first Welsh parliament for centuries at Machynlleth, and made treaties with the Scots, the French and the Pope. Even better from the point of view of those misty-eyed Celts who love to believe their heroes never really die but are waiting in the hills to return and free them from the English yoke, Owain disappeared some time around 1412 and was never seen again.

Unless, of course, you care to believe that he was reincarnated as Neil Kinnock!

There's a modern Mummers' Play which I came across recently which uses Owain and Lord Grey as its main characters. Here's how it starts:

Narrator picks OWAIN GLYDWR. He is the people's hero. He was responsible for reform of the Church, the establishment of Welsh Universities, and the burning down of the Ruthin Conservative Club.

Cheer Leader: The people CHEER when they hear OWAIN GLYNDWR'S name. (CHEER!).

Narrator: OWAIN GLYNDWR (CHEER!) had a confident swagger. Pick SIR REGINALD GREY OF RUTHIN. The villain of this story is the Marcher Lord SIR REGINALD GREY OF

> *RUTHIN. A dastardly scoundrel and member of the Ruthin Conservative Club.*

> *Cheer Leader: The people BOO when they hear SIR REGINALD GREY OF RUTHIN'S name. (BOO!).*

> *Narrator: Whenever SIR REGINALD GREY OF RUTHIN (BOO!) walked, he walked with a pronounced limp. (Let him limp). No, he walked with a pronounced limp wrist! He always pronounced the letter "R" as the letter "W". They called him SIR WEGINALD GWEY OF WIFFIN (BOO!)*

And maybe that's a better way to remember all of this last rebellion of the Welsh against the English - better at any rate than burning down English holidaymakers' cottages.

One of the highlights (literally) of St Peter's Square is the unusual set of seven dormer windows set into the roof of the sixteenth century Myddleton Arms, now rebadged, appropriately, as Seven Eyes. These are known as "The Eyes of Ruthin" and from them you can almost certainly see, or at least imagine you can see, most of the other sights in this attractive little town. Immediately opposite, in front of the mock Tudor Exmewe Hall, now occupied inevitably by Barclays Bank, is an unprepossessing limestone boulder which allegedly is where King Arthur beheaded Huail, the son of Kaw.

Who? I can hear you ask. Why? I hear your plaintive cry. And do we really need to know? Well, you can skip this section if you really want to but, if you do, you probably won't do very well in your *I Spy Wales* quiz book, so it's up to you.

Now Arthur was actually a bit of a randy old dog, as was the way of those old kings, and he spread his favours around generously. One babe that he was carrying on with was two-timing him with Huail and, when Arthur found out, he lost his cool and challenged Huail to a duel. They fought and Huail prevailed, wounding Arthur in the thigh, which gave him a slight limp for ever after (and I don't mean a limp wrist!). There was then a reconciliation and, because Arthur was king and could insist on such things, he made Huail promise never to reveal the result of this fight, on penalty of losing his head.

Some time after this Arthur was spreading it around again and was having a bit of a ding-dong with another babe in Ruthin. In order to spend more time with her, Arthur indulged in a bit of cross-dressing, disguising himself as a woman, and while dancing with this lady and her companions, he was spotted by Huail who noticed the lameness and remarked:

"This dancing might do very well, but for the thigh."

Strong stuff, eh? Arthur, of course, overheard this and gave Huail a bit of a bollocking for breaking his word. And then he had him beheaded on a stone - that very same stone, allegedly, called Maen Huail that attracts dogs outside Barclays Bank to this day.

Some people will believe anything!

Huail wasn't the only miscreant who spent time in Ruthin, for just downhill from "The Eyes of Ruthin", you'll come upon the old County Gaol, closed in 1916 but recently re-opened as the county record office, with rooms amusingly labelled Cell 1, Cell 2 *et cetera*, and as a rather splendid tourist attraction. Now, you might not think it a load of fun to go wandering around something as gruesome as an old gaol, but believe me there are some fascinating stories retold here, which make you think about the purposes of imprisonment.

My favourite is about Coch Bach, a.k.a. John Jones, a notorious thief and poacher from Bala who served sentences in every gaol in North Wales and in several in England. He was also a master escapologist, which earned him the nickname of "The Welsh Houdini". In 1913 he was sentenced to three years imprisonment in Bala for stealing from the local solicitor - not a good career move. And, although he did make his escape from there, he was soon recaptured and transferred to the supposedly more secure Ruthin Gaol. On the night before his transfer to HM Prison Stafford, Coch

Bach did another runner (the second time he'd liberated himself from Ruthin - you'd think they might have learned, wouldn't you?). His modus operandi on this occasion was to create a hole in his cell wall, through which he climbed out, using his bedclothes tied together in the time-honoured tradition of comedy films. Sadly for those of us who have a sneaking admiration for such roguery but happily for the local PC Plodwyns, who must have become fed up of constantly chasing him, this was Coch Bach's last escape. After five days on the run he was discovered and, in trying to escape, was shot in the leg and died of shock. He was buried locally and such was his notoriety that postcards of his burial were on sale shortly afterwards and did a roaring trade.

Then there's the tale of the last man to be hanged in Ruthin Gaol, a certain William Hughes, whose end came in February 1903. Hughes, a Wrexham miner, was found guilty of shooting his wife, from whom he had separated some time previously. She had apparently placed her two sons in the workhouse and gone to live with a man named Thomas Maddocks, claiming she was his housekeeper, though Hughes thought there was more to it than that, if you get my drift. The poor miner was then imprisoned for a month for not paying towards the upkeep of his two sons and, when he came out of prison, he was, as you can imagine, pretty fired up. He bought a shotgun and set off, intending to blast holes in his wife and Maddocks. The later had the good sense to be on the night shift so the ex-wife got both barrels. Hughes then gave himself up and his own life ended shortly afterwards.

When you walk around the abandoned cells, with their clever modern gadgetry bringing back what it must have been like to be imprisoned there, it does make you think about the whole prison regime. There has been an explosion in the numbers of people convicted and sent to prison in the United Kingdom in recent years, as successive Home Secretaries have executed their knee-jerk reaction to the popular press's constant braying about how unsafe it is to be alive today. Is there really more crime today than in the past? Are today's criminals really much tougher than those of yesteryear? And why do so many prisoners re-offend so soon after their release? I'm not sure of the answers to any of these questions but I do feel that they need asking, and asking again and again. A society that seeks to be thought of as fair and inclusive of all maybe has to find other ways of dealing with some of those of its members who are deviants from the straight and narrow.

Oh dear, that all sounds rather preacherly, doesn't it? So let's end this section with a lighter moment.

Another prisoner in Ruthin Gaol, commonly known as Dai the Thief, received a letter one day from his wife.

"I have decided to plant some vegetables in the back garden. When is the best time to plant them?" it read.

Dai, knowing that the prison guards read all mail, replied in a letter:

"Dear wife, whatever you do, do not touch the back garden. That is where I hid all the money."

A week or so later, he received another letter from his wife.

"You won't believe what happened. Some men came with shovels to the house, and dug up all the back garden."

Dai then wrote another letter:

"Dear wife, now is the best time to plant the vegetables."

Ruthin Castle, which Owen Glendower failed to destroy, was originally a Welsh fortress made of wood and stone but was taken over and later enlarged by the Anglo-Norman invaders. Successive members of the nobility inhabited it until the time of the Civil War when it was attacked and virtually turned into a ruin by the Republican troops of Major General Mytton. It was rebuilt in the Victorian era and made to look like a medieval castle again, which is presumably why Best Western came to purchase it and use it as a hotel, complete with romantic ruins and peacocks in the gardens. But prior to the First World War it was inhabited by George Cornwallis-West and his wife Jennie, the mother of Winston Churchill. The beautiful Jennie Jerome, born in Brooklyn of a mother who was one-quarter Iroquois Indian, was one of the few tattooed women in high society, with a snake coiled around her left wrist. She married Lord Randolph Churchill and gave birth to Winston but was known as a glamorous figure in society, described thus by a contemporary:

> *"She was still, in middle age, the mistress of many hearts, and the Prince of Wales (later Edward VII) was known to delight in her company. Her grey eyes sparkled with the joy of living and when, as was often the case, her anecdotes were risqué it was with her eyes as well as her words that one could read the implications. She was an accomplished pianist, an intelligent and well-informed reader and an enthusiastic advocate of any novelty."*

Lady Churchill had a lively correspondence with many distinguished persons. When she invited Bernard Shaw to lunch he replied with a telegram:

"Certainly not: What have I done to provoke such an attack on my well-known habit?"

Sir Winston's mother replied:"Know nothing of your habits; hope they are not as bad as your manners."

Her marriage to Cornwallis-West, following the death of Randolph Churchill, did not last long but, while they were together, Ruthin Castle was the scene of much riotous living by the rich and powerful, the latter-day Lord Greys.

Nowadays, as well as providing very expensive accommodation, Ruthin Castle offers medieval banquets, whose current menu I reproduce for you below:

FIRST - Cawl Crochan
SECOND - Asen Cig Oen
THIRD - Cym Rhostio Mewn Gwin Cymysgfwyd o Lysiau Gardd
FOURTH - Hufen Cloch y Gwin

Puzzling, eh? Don't worry. All you need to know is that the first course is veggie soup, the second is lamb (Welsh, of course), the third is chicken with a jacket potato, and the fourth is a fruit syllabub. Easy, isn't it? And the whole thing is accompanied by copious quantities of mead or wine and includes entertainment from "our court sheriff and his ladies of the court" while you listen to "beautiful harp music and singing in the candlelight" in the company of the "baron and baroness". And all of this will set you back a mere £31.95.

Tempting, eh?

I wonder if Rhys Ifans ever attended the medieval banquet, for the comic actor, the surprise star of the Hugh Grant - Julia Roberts film *Notting Hill* and then hailed by Entertainment weekly magazine as "one of Hollywood's hottest comedy imports" comes from Ruthin. There he was known as Gerry Evans and is remembered in the local school as "notorious" but "fondly remembered". We remember him as Hugh Grant's hygienically-challenged flatmate Spike and in particular that embarrassing scene when he opens the door of their London flat, wearing nowt but his Y-fronts, to be greeted by the London paparazzi.

Ifans / Evans began acting in school then joined the local youth theatre. Professional life began as one half of comedy duo the Two Franks (no, I've never heard of them either), and at one time he was briefly a member of Welsh rock n' roll band Super Furry Animals. He then won a role in a cult movie *Twin Town*, before landing the part of Spike in *Notting Hill*. Subsequently, he has co-starred with Robert Carlisle in *Once Upon a Time in the Midlands* and with Kevin Spacey and Judy Dench in *The Shipping News*.

Ifans / Evans has strong views about Welsh nationalism and would have been, I suspect, happy to be a member of Owen Glendower's troops, setting fire to his native Ruthin. He has a certain charisma on the screen which is why he's so popular with movie directors. But I suspect many of you, like me, will remember him for a long time for that abiding image of Spike in his grey undies - a Taff in pants.

And I suppose, if his career should ever go backwards, he could always get a part entertaining the hordes at Ruthin Castle's medieval banquets.

19 Ruthin to Prestatyn

I was joined at breakfast the following morning by a middle-aged couple named Alan and Moira whom I had not seen the previous evening. After the usual initial pleasantries were exchanged, I remarked that it was the first time I had heard Welsh spoken on my journey by the young couple with the child who had been sitting near me in the bar the night before.

"Yes, you can expect to hear more Welsh up here than in the valleys where we come from," said Alan. "This was always the Welsh heartland. Of course, in the valleys in the south industrialisation brought in a lot of migrants and that killed off the language."

"The English again?" I asked smiling.

"And the Irish. And the Scots," Alan replied. "Coal and steel brought them flocking in."

"Hasn't the education system been good for keeping the language alive?" I asked.

"Yes, it has done that," agreed Alan.

"But the problem is when they leave school and start work, the young people find themselves in an environment where they have to use English and they forget quickly their Welsh roots," added Moira.

"Yes, it's very worrying. The last census showed that the numbers of Welsh speakers is declining in some places," said Alan.

It is amazing in many ways that the Welsh language has survived so strongly at all. An Act of Parliament passed in Henry VIII's time annexed Wales into England and forbade the appointment of any Welsh speaker to any office or to any landowning position. Despite the efforts of determined groups of Dais and Owains to hold on to their language and culture, it was still the case in early Victorian times that Anglican ministers appointed to Welsh churches did not have to speak any Welsh. It was even worse in the schools. A government report of the mid-19th century declared:

> *"The Welsh language is a vast drawback to Wales and a manifold barrier to the moral progress and commercial prosperity of the people. It is not easy to overestimate its evil effects."*

Of course, things are better now, thanks to organisations like the Welsh Language Society and Plaid Cymru who have campaigned over the years to give their own language proper status. Nowadays all children attending school in Wales have to learn Welsh and a quarter of all Welsh schools teach a large part of their curriculum in Welsh. Progress is slow but real, for in the twenty years since the 1981 census the Welsh-speaking population has risen from 19% to 28%.

So maybe I should have watched Telewele in Llangollen the night I was there, rather than lamenting the fact that I couldn't see Rod Hull and Emu.

That day's walking was another of those special days. The weather was grand - hazy sun, blue sky, warm breeze - and the scenery was spectacular. There was an initial climb up the sides of first Moel Eithinen and then, after a short descent, of Moel Fenlii with its Iron Age hillfort. This was supposedly once occupied by a local bigwig who fell foul of the tongue of St Germanus, sent by the Pope to help ensure that the true faith was being followed in Wales. As a result of this falling out, the settlement on Moel Fenlii was burned down, though later writers suspect this was more likely the result of dodgy cooking practices on the barbecue than of spontaneous combustion.

Not far from here is the site of a famous battle featuring St Germanus, who wore the same hood and tunic in all seasons, and slept on ashes in a framework of boards, and the Irish invaders from the west who were not true believers (this was before *Father Ted*, of course). The story goes that Germanus, then a mere bishop but in a previous life a military commander, offered to lead the Welsh and Saxon army against the invader. He deployed his troops around the sides of a valley called Maes Garmon and lay in ambush, waiting for the enemy. At Germanus' signal, the troops all shouted "Hallelujah" in unison, and the sound frightened the Irish into a panicked retreat. A contemporary account records it thus:

"...and the great cry rebounded, shut in by the surrounding hills. The enemy column was terrified; the very frame of heaven and the rocks around seemed to threaten them...they fled in all directions"

The battle of Maes Garmon has come to be known as the Hallelujah Victory. Nice one, eh? D'you think I might beat off the enemy if I deployed my troops to shout "Bugger Offa!" I don't think so, do you?

After half-ascending Foel Fenlii, the Path veers left and takes you on a splendid walk around the contours of the hill and then down to a car park where a notice board informs you about the Moel Famau Country Park. The path ahead of you stretches clearly from the car park up to the Jubilee Tower on the top of Moel Famau and the notice board suggests that it will take you forty minutes to walk there. I did it in thirty.

The Tower was built to celebrate the jubilee of George III, the mad king, who was seventy-two at the time. There was a film called *The Madness of George III*, based on a stage play written by Alan Bennett, which was nominated for several Oscars a few years back, although this was after it had had to be retitled *The Madness of King George* because American audiences thought it was some sort of sequel like *Rocky III*. The witty film tells the story of George III, not the first or the last monarch to be loony, who talked to the trees and did other strange things like fancying the pants off women other than his wife. It all sounds worrying like our own dear Prince Charlie, doesn't it?

The original plan of the tower was for a three-stage obelisk rising some 160 feet into the heavens but there were considerable difficulties carrying large blocks of stone 2,000 feet up the hillside and then the money ran out before it had been finished. The foundation stone was laid in 1810 and for nearly fifty years it must have been a towering, even though unfinished, monument on the Clwydian landscape. Sadly a gigantic storm in 1862 blew it down and no one had the cash or the wherewithal to rebuild it. Later the top tiers were demolished to make it safe, leaving the stumpy bottom as the only survivor.

In more recent times a series of toposcopes has been added inside the tower and on this clearest of clear days I was able with their help to pick out Snowdon, Cader Idris, Liverpool Bay and the distant sea, as well as Ruthin in the Vale of Clwyd below. It was truly spectacular to stand there, with the gentle breeze wafting through my hair, gazing into the distance to see these landmarks.

Moel Famau, together with two other local hills, Pen Machno and Moel Dwyll, was the unlikely scene of a gold rush back in the 1880s. The gold found in the mines hereabouts was reputed to be the finest in Wales and many a miner set off by horse and cart from the nearby village of Cilcain, visible from the Jubilee Tower, to seek his fortune in them thar hills. It didn't last long, however, for the mines were closed in 1895 as being uneconomic, so the miners returned to doing what they had done before. And in Cilcain's case this was pretty unpleasant, for the village had a reputation for the amount of cock-fighting, brawling and drinking that went on there. Maybe that's why it was chosen as the site for *Hilary and Jackie*, the film about cellist Jacqueline du Pré who led a very racy life herself until she was sadly struck down with illness.

From Moel Famau there followed a hill walk to equal the one on Hatterall Ridge that I had so much enjoyed on the first week of my trek, though there were more dips and rises this time. Again the ground was springy underfoot and the way was easy and again I was accompanied all the way by a plethora of birds, this time meadow pipits with their distinctive call rather than skylarks. So I marched easily over Moel Dywyll and Moel Llys-y-Coed and down to yet another car park at the bottom of Moel Arthur, where I caught up with Dave, a recently-retired Ford engineer who had been walking the whole Offa's Dyke path in one go and camping en route. I could see he was struggling up hills so I waited for him when I could and, when we reached the summit of Moel Arthur, we stopped for lunch.

I've already told you about the tradition in Llangollen and some other parts of North Wales for processions to go to the top of the nearest mountain on Easter Day. Well there's another tradition for gangs of Doris Dancers to do the same thing on May Day. Except that they don't make do with three somersaults. Oh no, they go for the full Monty, don't they? There was a group who went up Moel Arthur a few years ago, sixteen goodly souls wearing their distinctive blacked faces, top hats and tails to emphasise their abundant red, yellow and green ribbons, and the unique motifs on their backs. There, at four thirtyish in the morning as the sun was rising, they launched into their repertoire with dances bearing names even stranger than their costumes - Craven Stomp, Ragged Crow, Hunt the Dragon, and for their *pièce de resistance* Not for Joe.

Is it just me or are these guys completely loony? Though, on second thoughts, I have to say it still makes more sense than skateboarding or collecting teddy bears.

Moel Arthur, as you might expect, is so called because of its alleged links to King Arthur and there's the usual collection of stories and suppositions explaining those links. Some argue that the valley below the hill was actually the site of Camelot, others that it was the site of the Battle of Camlann. To be honest, I'm not sure Arthur ever existed but this last link with him gives me the opportunity to tell one final legend about him.

Arthur was preparing to go on a Quest that would take him away from Camelot for a long time and he was worried about leaving Queen Guinevere alone with all those randy Knights of the Round Table. So he went to Merlin for some advice. The good wizard showed him his latest invention - a chastity belt that had large hole in it.

"This is no good, Merlin!" Arthur exclaimed, "Look at this opening. How is this supposed to protect the Queen?"

"Ah, sire, just observe," said Merlin as he selected his most worn-out wand and inserted it in the gaping aperture of the chastity belt, whereupon a small guillotine blade came down and cut it neatly in two.

"Merlin, you are a genius!" said the grateful monarch, "Now I can leave, knowing that my Queen is fully protected."

After putting Guinevere in the device, King Arthur then set out upon his Quest. Several years passed until he returned to Camelot.

Immediately he assembled all his knights in the courtyard and had them drop their trousers for an informal inspection. Sure enough! Each and every one of them was either amputated or damaged in some way. All of them except Galahad.

"Sir Galahad," exclaimed King Arthur, "The one and only true knight! Only you among all the nobles have been true to me. What is it in my power to grant you? Name it and it is yours!"

But, alas, Sir Galahad was speechless.

It turned out that Dave and I were both staying at Fron Haul near to Bodfari that night, so we walked together for the rest of that afternoon. As I mentioned earlier, Dave was camping along the route, which meant he was carrying tent, sleeping bag and cooking gear as well as the change of clothes that was pretty much all I was carrying. In order to keep his weight to a minimum, Dave was not carrying Ordnance Survey maps but just the strip maps and notes of the route issued by the Offa's Dyke Association. This meant that he had no idea of the geography or topography of his journey, other than of that immediately adjacent to the Path. So when I pointed out Snowdon to him that evening, he was utterly gobsmacked. Because of the weight he was carrying and the consequent limitations on his speed, he also tended to go to bed early and set off early in the morning. This meant he never went to the pub in the evening. It did not sound like much fun to me.

Fron Haul is a smashing place, used by Offa's Dykers ever since the Path was first opened back in 1971. It is a highly unusual Victorian house, built originally for a wealthy surgeon, and one of its most unusual features is that it has a number of balconies giving outstanding views over the Vale of Clwyd and the mountains beyond. Fron Haul is situated on the hillside above Bodfari in a tiny settlement called Sodom, though I have no idea why this delightful place should bear such an unpleasant name. The house is the sort of place where you feel you have been given free reign in someone's home and this is all down to Gladwys Edwards whose home it is. A keen walker herself, Gladwys is the only person I stayed with on my walk who knows what walking the Offa's Dyke Path really entails. And she makes wonderful raspberry jam. And she had taken it on herself to book me a table at the Downing Arms in Bodfari that evening.

I was sat outside in Gladwys's garden in the early Saturday evening sunlight, holding a desultory conversation with Dave as he sorted out the gear in his tent, when suddenly from nowhere my wife appeared.

"Bugger Offa!" I exclaimed.

"No," she said sternly. "You can't use that title."

"No, I mean what are you doing here?" I said.

"I thought I'd surprise you," she replied. "It was such a lovely day I thought I'd drive up to North Wales for the rest of the weekend and here I am. Aren't you pleased to see me?"

Of course I was. We tried to persuade Dave to join us but he wanted to get to bed so he could be off bright and early in the morning, so we went to the Downing Arms ourselves. It was wonderful to have my wife with me after a week away from home. And to get a lift to the pub and back - what a treat!

We returned with half a bottle of red wine, intending to sit out in the garden in the late evening to finish it off. My wife, though, was tired and went to bed, leaving me to finish the wine alone. As I sat there sipping among the whirring of the grasshoppers, the smell of raspberry jam, and the loopy flight of moths, it was hard not to feel at peace with the world. And then suddenly there came the sound of faint organ music. When I went to investigate,

I found that it was Gladwys's husband Derek sat behind two keyboards, playing a medley of 1950s hits. I sat down and tried to sing along to the Doris Day selection but all I knew was *Que Sera Sera*, which we managed to finish more or less together. I requested the Beatles and Derek made a brave stab at *All My Loving*. Fortunately, or so my wife said later, he did not know my party piece, *Blueberry Hill*.

It was a bizarre end to a wonderful evening in Sodom. And tomorrow?

Sunday, the final day of my journey on Offa's Dyke Path, began like so many others with a climb, this time up a hill called Cefn Du. As I climbed I caught occasional glimpses of St Asaph over to the west with its cathedral whose stained glass windows tell the story of its foundation. Apparently Queen Nest, the most beautiful woman in Wales, while skinny-dipping in the River Elwy dropped her antique gold wedding ring into the water. So she went to ask Bishop Asaph how she should tell her husband. That evening, while having some Welsh cakes with the couple down at the local caff, Bishop Asaph told the king, who was really brassed off, until Asaph did the Christian bit about love being greater than riches.

Then Asaph served Nest with a portion of a magnificent locally-caught salmon and, lo and behold, from the flesh with a loud tinkle the precious ring fell on to the table, thus completing a curious circular journey from finger to river to salmon and back home to Nest's finger.

Altogether now, aah!

By mid-morning I had come down from the Clwydian Hills, crossed the busy A55 which follows the line of the old Roman road from Chester to Holyhead, and reached the small town of Rhuallt. The Smithy Arms that I passed advertised itself as being open all day but not until midday on a Sunday. It was ten thirty in the morning as I strode through and who needs beer at that time of day anyway?

There's nothing spectacular to write home about on this final few miles of the Path, to tell the truth. It takes a pleasant enough route across fields, along quiet fly-infested lanes where waving my walking pole in front of me proved an excellent deterrent, and through leafy woods. But there's nothing that really hits you as remarkable until you climb through the gorse and scrub surrounding a disused quarry and suddenly you're out in the open, overlooking the horror of thousands of retirement bungalows in Prestatyn and beyond them the grey sea.

Down a narrow track you tread from the final height on this wonderful walk till you reach the open road and the entry to Prestatyn.

My journey was nearly at an end and I felt great.

20 Prestatyn

Philip Larkin once wrote a poem called Sunny Prestatyn, which begins like this:

Come to Sunny Prestatyn
Laughed the girl on the poster,
Kneeling up on the sand
In tautened white satin.

The poem takes an ironic look at the lies told by advertising techniques and how the reality, in the case of this poster its disfigurement by the local vandals and graffiti artists, is always much worse than we are led to believe. But still we want to believe and I entered Prestatyn hoping against hope that it would be even a tad better than my childhood remembrance of a North Wales seaside resort.

At first glance, Prestatyn appears to be a dump. But take a closer look and you'll see that it's worse than that. It has only one street worth the name, High Street, which begins, if you're entering from the south as I was, with two funeral parlours and goes downhill, literally and metaphorically, from there. I've never seen so many chip and kebab shops, so many charity shops, and so many cut-price goods shops anywhere in Britain. The town signage at the top of High Street should have warned me, for among its nine designated places of interest one is the beach, another is the beach gardens, another is the beach entertainment centre, and another is the promenade. We'll come to those in a second but I warn you now - don't hold your breath! The other enticements of Prestatyn are the hillside behind it, through which I had walked to conclude my journey, a three-mile cycle path on an old railway line, the parish church, dating as far back as the nineteenth century (now calm down, please!), and the Offa's Dyke Path itself. And having visited Prestatyn now, I am quite convinced that Offa never built his wall this far. Even he, ruthless monarch that he was, would have surely turned his nose up at what he found here. Oh, I've forgotten the Scala Cinema and Arts Centre, which bears a notice proclaiming its closure due to unforeseen circumstances, which I learned meant it was in a dangerous condition and falling apart.

It's no wonder Carol Vorderman couldn't wait to get out of Prestatyn, is it? The lovely Carol, the beautiful brainbox who made her name on the long-running TV quiz programme *Countdown* alongside Richard "Twice Nightly" Whiteley, spent her formative years in this jewel of the north Wales coastline. She is described as having an IQ which seems to vary between 154 or of 169, depending which fanzine you read, and is a member of MENSA; she is used by government agencies to promote maths teaching; and last year she was awarded the MBE for services to broadcasting, despite only getting a third-class degree in engineering at Cambridge.

Makes you think, eh?

Actually it's only in the last few years that La Vorderman has become a serious celebrity. She has been appearing on *Countdown* since it began in 1982, after being persuaded by her mother to apply for the number-crunching job advertised rather than remaining as a shop worker in Leeds. Over the years she has been promoted as being a bit of a know-it-all, even, some like to think, as the brainiest person on television. The transformation in her fortunes began with her decision to wear a revealing, low-cut, thigh-length, turquoise dress at the BAFTA Awards ceremony in 2000, thus showing off her new skinny figure (allegedly the result of imbibing nothing other than grass juice for several months) and being featured in just about every newspaper the following day. Before that she was a mumsy, size-14 brainbox who wore nice, sensible blouses, and knee-length skirts. Now she is one of television's favourite bits of eye candy, always fronting some dreadful new programme like *Better Homes* or *Better Budgie*

Cages or *Better Loos*, wearing spray-on leather trousers or PVC mini-skirts.

That dress and that transformation led to the break-up of her marriage, with her husband claiming that he was fed up with her constant late-night boozing and schmoozing and that the dress made her look tarty and him feel humiliated. As an indication of how famous she now is - and for nothing other than being a celebrity - in 2001 there were 758 major newspaper headlines about her, outmentioned only by the vile Anne Robinson. More encouragingly for us mere mortals is the fact that in the same year she won the "Worst Celebrity Haircut" title, beating such luminaries as Bob Geldof, Ann Widdecombe and Victoria Beckham.

Treading a path made familiar by other skinny female celebs, Carol produced her own dieting video last year, in which she gives advice on how you (or me for that matter, if I were daft enough to believe her) can lose loads of weight in 28 days and end up looking like her. It's called *Carol Vorderman's 28 Day Detox Diet* and here's what one happy customer, who was so enthused by it that she wrote it on the internet, thought of it:

> *This video did not help me AT ALL! I'm still eating as much junk food as ever but can no longer watch my favourite programme Countdown as I keep remembering how patronising she really is. Just accept that you're fat and ugly, no video will change this. Spend the money on chocolate instead.*

Good advice, if you ask me. And just in case you think I'm being too hard on the voluptuous number-cruncher, let me state here and now that I too have a third class degree and you will know from reading these pages that they could not have been written by anyone who was not a genius. So:

"Give me a consonant, Carol."

'Nuff said.

One of the curiosities about Prestatyn is that it was once, in the early days of moving pictures, the home of a cinematographer called Saronie. This pioneering gentleman, originally plain James Roberts, showed the first movie in north Wales in 1899. It was advertised thus - *Animated Photography, The Greatest Wonder of the Nineteenth Century. The entertainment will include talks, songs and whistles.* You do wonder about those whistles, don't you? What ever happened to whistling? It used to be such a common pastime but what do young people do now? Skateboard or drink Bacardi Breezers. It's no wonder the world is going to the dogs.

Sorry, old fart prejudices coming out again. Will have to get them back under control.

Saronie started his career in films at Birkenhead where he made two-minute films of local events and showed them at the Coliseum. After being shown, these films were then rushed by cyclists at breakneck speed to his other cinema at the Park in Tranmere. These early films, shown to an enthralled public, were of such exciting things as the launching of a ship from Camell Laird's Shipyards, soldiers embarking for the Boer War, and the visit of the Prince of Wales to Ruthin.

Wow!

In 1910, Saronie began showing films in the Town Hall at Prestatyn which he soon converted into a cinema. There Saronie's World Famous Electric Pictures went on show twice weekly. By now he was known as, "The only, as well as the pioneer, cinematographist in North Wales". By 1915 he was showing films of war pictures direct from the front that would "appeal to everyone with patriotic instincts", and that same year saw the showing of the first colour film in Prestatyn, described as, "A three part Drama in nature's colours entitled *A Queen's Love*". In 1930 the first talkie, advertised as "A great hundred per cent talking picture for three days only, Glen Tryon in Broadway. Original play dialogue with songs, gorgeous dance numbers, gaiety runs riot, spectacular scenes, big cast", was shown by Saronie at the Scala.

Saronie continued to run the Scala until 1963, when he retired and sold it to the local Council. But there, in that fascinating brief history, you have the history of the moving image from its earliest beginnings through to a time when it went into the doldrums. The impact of all those images from around the world being displayed before the citizens of this North Wales seaside resort can only be guessed at. One thing those images failed to do, however, was inspire them to create a better-looking town.

On my way to the beach and the final point on the long journey that had been Offa's Dyke Path I passed a pub near the railway station called Offa's Tavern. Well, I was tempted, I have to say. But I resisted, for the moment at least, and soon enough I was heading over the railway footbridge and on the very final stretch of my journey from sea to sea. And the seaside is what most people think of when you mention Prestatyn, for, as motorised transport grew in the inter-war years and with it ordinary people's capacity to travel for their holidays, so the beaches of North Wales became targets for the working class thousands of Liverpool and south-west Lancashire. The resort of Prestatyn grew accordingly and in fact it is really merged with nearby Rhyl on its coastal front, being separated by little more than a golf course.

The town's signage I've already mentioned as being dominated by the seaside so let me tell you a little more about the sites it nominates. The Nova Entertainment Centre, where the Beatles once played before fame took them to higher things, situated right at the centre of the beach complex, contains a swimming pool, bars, a restaurant and a fitness suite. The nearby Ffrith Festival Gardens offer fun rides and a miniature boating pool in addition to the aforesaid gardens, while the promenade stretches from the western Ffrith Beach to the eastern Barkby Beach and it's at the latter I want to pause. For just by Barkby Beach is Pontin's Holiday Camp.

Now, be honest, you almost certainly thought that holiday camps had disappeared, didn't you? You thought all those Scouse scallies and their uneducated Ritas were swanning off to the Costa Lotta or the Greek Islands, didn't you? You didn't believe there could still be people in this day and age who chose to spend their holidays in a version of Colditz complete with blue-coated warders and the equivalent of NAAFI canteen food, did you? Well, you were wrong.

Ever since that wizard Billy Butlin created the first of these monstrosities at Skegness in 1936, the Brits have been patronising holiday camps. Their heyday was in the immediate post-war years, which was when Fred Pontin, a former London stockbroker, joined in the fun, opening Prestatyn camp and several others. And if you think that taking part in such inventive activities as 'Knobbly Knees' or 'Glamorous Grannies' competitions was none too exciting, just remember that there were also communal bathrooms with hot water, wire fences and ear-shattering loudspeaker announcements throughout the daytime. Maybe it was the military-barracks style that gave them their appeal, for of course in those post-war years men back from National Service had become used to that sort of thing.

Now Pontin's Prestatyn Holiday Camp is the very same place where that dire TV spin-off film *Holiday on the Buses* was filmed aeons ago. And, since I couldn't bear to enter the site (and, to be honest, I doubt if they would've allowed me past the Checkpoint Charlie barrier anyway), here's a bit of what one fan of this film wrote after revisiting recently:

Driving up to the old Pontins main gate and security hut felt very strange indeed. Good old-fashioned British Holiday camps have unfortunately had their day here in the UK. As a result, during the '80s and '90s, most have either closed down and been demolished, or renamed 'centres' - and changed so much that they are now totally unrecognisable.

But 'Holiday on the Buses' Pontins remains virtually identical to the 1973 celluloid! I quote, "you almost expect Blakey to be stood on guard at the gates!" Luckily, I didn't have to run the risk of bumping into "that" merry old soul as I found a hole in the rusty perimeter fence...

So what is it like? I managed to get a good look at all of the main buildings featured in the movie - the chalets, main reception, swimming pool, children's boating lake and first aid (!) block.

Remember when Jack and Stan first arrive at the camp? A fanfare is playing and people are literally swarming around the main reception building. These days things are rather more quiet! I saw two, maybe three people here. No Pontins open-top tour bus outside either. The reception gazebo had gone, as have the red and yellow paving stones. The front of the building has instead been clad in dark blue metal. However, the line of Pontins flags are still fluttering away.

There's more but, to be honest, I think I've had enough and I suspect you have too. I'm told on good authority that *Holiday on the Buses* is still the most frequently-watched film in Prestatyn - it's considered high art there. Which probably tells you all you need to know about the place. So let's leave Blakey, Jack and Stan, and good old Fred Pontin to their shenanigans. It was time to finally conclude my journey.

According to the official *Offa's Dyke Path North* guidebook, there is a walkers' tradition that you take your boots and socks off when you hit the beach at Prestatyn and wade into the sea, maintaining the line of the path, for as far out as you dare go. Excuse me! I thought to myself when I first read that. Do you really think, after walking 177 miles, I'm going to doff my boots for a silly stunt like that?

But I did. I got to Prestatyn earlier than I had expected and with time to spare before my wife arrived. So, even after strolling around the sights in Prestatyn town, even after detouring briefly to see Pontin's, I was left with time on my hands.

And so, as a weak sun struggled to warm the sad holiday-makers who insisted on sitting on the Central Beach with their curled-up sandwiches, their flasks of lukewarm tea, their plastic bathing rings and their Kiss-me-Kwik hats, I sat down to remove my socks and boots to let the fresh air get at my feet for the first time in over two weeks. In the time-honoured fashion of the British holidaymaker, I rolled up my trousers and strode into the salty water.

And as I waded through the cold waters of the Irish Sea, I thought of that bugger Offa, the self-styled King of the Angles, whose earthwork defined the boundaries of what he called Angle-land twelve centuries ago. What would he have done to celebrate? I wondered. Ordered a roast swan to be cooked up for him perhaps? Maybe a spitted boar or a grilled peacock? I'm sure he would have enjoyed several pints of honeyed mead to whet his whistle after building his great dyke.

I bet that, even if he had done as I had and set off in the freezing water in the direction of Ireland, he would have soon turned back to celebrate the end of his mighty task. And so that's what I did too. I turned back on myself, reshod myself, and headed back towards Prestatyn centre, where my wife was due to meet me. Soon I was ensconced in Offa's Tavern, tucking into a hearty repast of not swan but Walker's crisps and supping a pint not of mead but of Brains bitter.

I was not alone, for Johnny and Billy, two thirty-somethings who had been playing pool, had accosted me as I was waiting for my pint to arrive.

"Have you walked the Dyke?" Johnny, a longhaired guy with a cheesy grin, asked.

"Yes, just finished," I said proudly. "One hundred and seventy seven miles. It was brilliant."

"What? On your bike?" asked Billy, whose Scouse dialect was slurred from too many pints of lager.

"Does he look like he rides a bike?" interrupted Johnny, showing his disdain of his companion. "He's wearing boots."

"I couldn't do that," slurred Billy. "I could ride it, mind you. I could ride round the world, me. Any time. No problem."

He reached for the pool table to steady himself.

"You couldn't do anything," said Johnny. "You can't even beat me at pool. Anyway, mate, you've done brilliant. Here's to you."

They both lifted their glasses in salute and shook my hand, as if I were their best ever mate and they hadn't seen me for yonks.

And, as I raised my glass, I thought of the magnificent journey I had travelled for 177 miles up hill and down dale through the Marches; I thought of the fascinating characters I had met, both living and dead; and I thought especially of our great forebear from the Dark Ages, that mighty Mercian warrior, that builder of one of history's most remarkable boundaries, that very special Offa.

USEFUL READING INFORMATION

Anon (2000), *Report of the Task Force on Potentially Hazardous Near Earth Objects*, British National Space Centre

Anon (2002), *Ruthin Gaol: A Brief History*, Denbighshire County Council

Anon (2003), *Offa's Dyke Path - Where to Stay etc*, Offa's Dyke Association

Borrow, George (1923), *Wild Wales*, John Murray

Campbell, James; John, Eric & Wormald, Patrick (1991), *The Anglo-Saxons*, Penguin Books

Chatwin, Bruce (1996) *On the Black Hill*, Vintage

Clarke, Kate (2000), *The Book of Hay*, Logaston Press

Dircks, Will H. (ed.) (1888), *The Autobiography of Edward, Lord Herbert of Cherbury*, Walter Scott

Doyle, Sir Arthur Conan (1996), *The Hound of the Baskervilles*, Penguin Books

Evans, D.H. (1987), *Valle Crucis Abbey*, CADW

Evans, J.A.H. (2002), *Nathaniel Wells of Piercefield and St Kitts: From Slave to Sheriff*, Chepstow Museum

Hayter, William (1977), *Spooner - A Biography*, W.H. Allen

Higginbotham, John (undated), *Kington Camp*, Kington History Society

Hill, David & Worthington, Margaret (2003), *Offa's Dyke History and Guide*, Tempus Publishing Ltd

Hodges, Geoffrey (1955), *Owain Glyn Dwr: the War of Independence on the Welsh Borders*, Logaston Press

Hogg, Garry (1946), *...And Far Away*, Phoenix House Ltd

Housman, A.E. (2000), *A Shropshire Lad*, Penguin Books

Hunter, David (2001), *Walking Offa's Dyke Path*, Cicerone Press

Jones, Gwyn & Jones, Thomas (trans.) (1949), *The Mabinogion*, J.M. Dent

Kay, Ernie & Kathy & Richards, Mark (2000), *Offa's Dyke Path South*, Aurum Press

Kay, Ernie & Kathy & Richards, Mark (2001), *Offa's Dyke Path North*, Aurum Press

Kerr, Douglas (ed.) (1994), *The Works of Wilfred Owen*, Wordsworth Editions

Lloyd, J.D.K (1984), *Montgomery Guidebook*, Montgomery Civic Society

Lovegrove, Roger (1990), *The Kite's Tale: The Story of the Red Kite in Wales*, RSPB

Mavor, Elizabeth (1973), *The Ladies of Llangollen*, Penguin Books

Miles, Jonathan (1952), *Eric Gill and David Jones at Capel-y-Ffin*, Siren Books

Phillips, Graham & Keatman, Martin (1992), *King Arthur - The True Story*, Random House

Plomer, William (ed.) (1978*), Kilvert's Diary 1870-1879*, Book Club Associates

Protz R. (ed.) (2003), *Good Beer Guide 2003*, CAMRA

Pym, Barbara (1980), *Excellent Women*, Penguin Books

Pym, Barbara (1980), *The Sweet Dove Died*, Granada Publishing Ltd

Stenton, Frank (1971), *Anglo-Saxon England*, Oxford University Press

Swanton, Michael (ed.) (2000), *The Anglo-Saxon Chronicle*, Phoenix Press

Thorpe, Lewis (trans.) (1966), *Geoffrey of Monmouth : The History of the Kings of Britain*, Penguin Books

Thorpe, Lewis (trans.) (1978), *Gerald of Wales: The Journey through Wales & The Description of Wales*, Penguin Books

Turner, Rick (2002), *Chepstow Castle*, CADW

Watkins, Alfred (1974), *The Old Straight Track*, Sphere Books

Williams, Raymond (1978), *Border Country*, Chatto and Windus

Zaluckyj, Sarah (2001), *Mercia: The Anglo-Saxon Kingdom of Central England*, Logaston Press

USEFUL TRAVEL INFORMATION

The best and most up-to-date information about the Offa's Dyke Path is obtainable from:

Offa's Dyke Association
West Street
Knighton
LD7 1EN

Tel: 01547-528753
Email: oda@offasdyke.demon.co.uk

TOURIST INFORMATION OFFICES

CHEPSTOW
Bridge Street, Chepstow, NP16 5EY
Tel: 01291-623772

MONMOUTH
Shire Hall, Agincourt Square, Monmouth, NP5 3DY
Tel: 01600-713899

ABERGAVENNY
Swan Meadow, Cross Street, Abergavenny, NP7 5HH
Tel: 01873-857588

HAY-ON-WYE
Craft Centre, Oxford Road, Hay-on-Wye, HR3 5AE
Tel: 01497-820144

KINGTON
2 Mill Street, Kington, Herefordshire, HR3 3BQ
Tel: 01544-230778

KNIGHTON
Offa's Dyke Centre, West Street, Knighton, LD7 1EW
Tel: 01547-529424

WELSHPOOL
Vicarage Garden, church Street, Welshpool, SY21 4JA
Tel: 01938-552043

OSWESTRY
Heritage Centre, Church Terrace, Oswestry, SY11 4JA
Tel: 01691-662753

LLANGOLLEN
Town Hall, Castle street, Llangollen, LL20 5PD
Tel: 01978-860828

RUTHIN
Craft Centre, Park Road, Ruthin, LL15 1BB
Tel: 01824-703992

PRESTATYN
Offa's Dyke Centre, Central Beach, Prestastyn, LL19 7EY
Tel: 01745-889092

MAPS

1:50,000 Ordnance Survey Landranger Series
  162 Gloucester & Forest of Dean
  161 The Black Mountains
  148 Presteigne & Hay-on-Wye
  137 Church Stretton & Ludlow
  126 Shrewsbury & Oswestry
  117 Chester & Wrexham
  116 Denbigh & Colwyn Bay

1:25,000 Ordnance Survey Explorer Series
  14 Wye Valley & Forest of Dean
  13 Brecon Beacons National Park   Eastern Area
  201 Knighton Presteigne
  216 Welshpool & Montgomery
  240 Oswestry
  256 Wrexham & Llangollen
  265 Clwydian Range / Bryniau

PLACES TO VISIT

CHEPSTOW CASTLE
Bridge Street, Chepstow, NP16 5EY
Tel: 01291-624065

CHEPSTOW MUSEUM
Bridge Street, Chepstow, NP6 5EZ
Tel: 01291-625981

TINTERN ABBEY
Tintern
Tel: 01291-689251

KYMIN NAVAL TEMPLE
Kymin Hill, Monmouth, NP25 3SD
Tel: 01600-719241

NELSON MUSEUM, MONMOUTH
Priory Street, Monmouth, NP25 3XA
Tel: 01600-710630

WHITE CASTLE
Llantilio Crossenny, Abergavenny, NP7 8UD
Tel: 01600-780380

SKIRRID INN
Llanfihangel Crucorney, Abergavenny, NP7 8DH
Tel: 01873-890258

LLANTHONY ABBEY
Llanthony, Abergavenny, NP7 7NN
Tel: 01873-890487

BOOTH BOOKS, HAY-ON-WYE
44 Lion Street, Hay-on-Wye, HR3 5AA
Tel: 01497-820322

HERGEST CROFT GARDENS
Hergest Estate, Kington, HR5 3EG
Tel: 01544-230160

KINGTON MUSEUM
Mill Street, Kington, HR5 3AL
Tel: 07974-526397

JUDGE'S LODGING, PRESTEIGNE
Broad Street, Presteigne, LD8 2AD
Tel: 01544-260650

SPACEGUARD CENTRE, KNIGHTON
Llanshay Lane, Knighton, LD7 1LW
Tel: 01547-520247

OFFA'S DYKE CENTRE, KNIGHTON
West Street, Knighton, LD7 1EW
Tel: 01547-529424

OLD BELL MUSEUM, MONTGOMERY
Arthur Street, Montgomery
Tel: 01686-668313

OSWESTRY HERITAGE CENTRE
Church Terrace, Oswestry, SY11 4JA
Tel: 01691-662753

CHIRK CASTLE
Chirk, Wrexham, LL14 5AF
Tel: 01691-777701

PLAS NEWYDD, LLANGOLLEN
Hill Street, Llangollen, LL20 8AW
Tel: 01978-861314

VALLE CRUCIS ABBEY
Llangollen, LL20 8DD
Tel: 01978-860326

RUTHIN GAOL
46 Clwyd Street, Ruthin, LL15 1HP
Tel: 01824-708250

ST ASAPH CATHEDRAL
High Street, St. Asaph, LL17 0AX
Tel: 01745-583429

OFFA'S DYKE CENTRE, PRESTATYN
Central Beach, Prestastyn, LL19 7EY
Tel: 01745-889092

USEFUL DRINKING INFORMATION

I am often asked for more information about the beers I sampled on my journey, so I have included details of most of those mentioned in this book.

Berkeley: Early Riser (4.8%)

Berkeley's Brewery is a small operation that began life in an old cider cellar in Berkeley, Gloucestershire, in 1996. Other beers include Dicky Pearce's Winter Ale and Lord's Prayer.

Brains: Reverend James Original Ale (4.5%)

The Reverend James is named after the founder of Buckleys Brewery, now absorbed within Brains Brewery of Cardiff. Buckleys Brewery began in 1767, when Henry Child, a strong Methodist, started to brew beer in Llanelli. The Reverend James Buckley later took on the serious development of the brewery after his marriage to Henry Child's daughter.

Breconshire Brewery: Rambler's Ruin (5%)

The Breconshire Brewery was founded in 2002, as a part of C.H. Marlow, a wholesaler and distributor of ales in the South Wales area for over 30 years. Head Brewer Justin 'Buster' Grant joined the company following the demise of Brakspears in Henley on Thames.

Cains: Dr Duncan (3.5%)

Liverpool's Robert Cain Brewery began in 1850 but has since been in the hands of other brewery chains like Boddingtons and Whitbread, though it has now reverted to its original name. Dr Duncan was the first Medical Officer for Health in Liverpool - an appropriate man to name a beer after.

Freeminer: Speculation Ale (4.8%)

The Freeminer Brewery, located in the Forest of Dean in Gloucestershire, is a recent addition to the real ale cause, being founded in 1992. It names its beers after terms used in the extensive mining in the Royal Forest of Dean. Speculation Ale is named after a mine originally opened by two Oxfordshire bankers.

Hook Norton: Old Hooky (4.6%)

The Hook Norton Brewery of Banbury can be traced back to 1849 when maltster John Harris set up in business. Much of the original brewing equipment is still in use and water is drawn from wells underneath the brewery.

Jennings: Cocker Hoop (4.8%)

Jennings Brewery of Cockermouth celebrated its 175th year of existence in 2003. Other beers produced include the wonderfully-named Sneck Lifter and Cross Buttock.

J.W. Lees: Scorcher (4.2%)

The family-owned J.W. Lees Brewery of Manchester had been brewing for 175 years in 2003. Its northwestern base allowed it to expand into north Wales many years ago. J.W. Lees also provides the beers for *Coronation Street's* Rover's Return pub. Scorcher is its summertime speciality.

Morland: Old Speckled Hen (5.2%)

Originally brewed by Morland of Abingdon, Old Speckled Hen is now made in Bury St Edmunds, Suffolk, by Greene King. The name comes from the name "owld speckled 'un", a term used to describe an old MG car covered with flecks of paint used as a runaround at the Abingdon-based MG company.

Shepherd Neame: Bishop's Finger (5%)

Kent's Shepherd Neame Brewery is reputedly the oldest continuous brewer in the country, dating back to 1698, though brewing has taken place on the site from the 12th century. A Bishops Finger is an unusual finger-shaped signpost still found in Kent, which once pointed pilgrims on their way to Canterbury.

Charles Wells: Bombardier (4.3%)

The Bedford-based brewery is the oldest independent family-owned brewery in the country. It was established in 1876 and is still run by the same family. Bombardier is currently being marketed as "England's Premier Pint" alongside a campaign to give greater status to St George's Day.

Wood: Special Bitter (4.2%)

Beginning in 1980, this Shropshire brewery, based in Craven Arms, has expanded over the years and produces an array of seasonal and occasional beers, including Hell for Leather, Get Knotted, Hopping Mad and Shropshire Lad.

PLACES TO EAT & DRINK

CHEPSTOW

Coach and Horses, Welsh Street
Tel: 01291-622626
Good traditional pub with a split-level interior, serving real ales. Summer beer festival coincides with Chepstow Festival. Near to racecourse and castle.

Boat Inn, The Back
Tel: 01291-628192
Atmospheric and popular riverside pub with excellent views of the Wye. Excellent food served throughout the week, including Sundays.

CHEPSTOW TO MONMOUTH

Boat Inn, Lone Lane, Penalt
Tel: 01600-712615
On side of River Wye, lovely dark old pub, serving real ales and home-made food. Wonderful atmosphere. Worth crossing the river for.

MONMOUTH

Green Dragon Inn, St. Thomas's Square
Tel: 01600-712561
Just beyond medieval Monmow Bridge, a comfortable pub that appeals to gentlemen of a certain temperament. Jazz on Wednesdays.

King's Head, Agincourt Square
Tel: 01600-713417
One of the town's former coaching hotels is now owned by Wetherspoons, who provide a range of good real ales and cheap food. Typical Wetherspoons but well done for all that.

MONMOUTH TO HAY-ON-WYE

Hunter's Moon Inn, Llangattock Lingoed
Tel: 01873-821499
Now the only pub on the Offa's Dyke Path between Monmouth and Pandy. Check for opening times.

Skirrid Inn, Hereford Road, Llanfihangel Crucorney
Tel: 01873-890258
Oldest pub in Wales and second oldest in the UK. The beer's nothing to write home about but the atmosphere is.

Lancaster Arms, Old Hereford Road, Pandy
Tel: 01873-890699
Welcoming, if slightly bizarre, pub. Unusual beers and pub grub. Worth going just to meet the landlord.

HAY-ON-WYE

Old Black Lion, Lion Street
Tel: 01497-820841
Probably the best place to eat in Hay-on-Wye. First-class menu and a lovely dining room, though you'll probably need to book.

Three Tuns, 4 Broad Street
No phone
A unique pub with a unique landlady. You won't get any ice-cold lagers in here but you simply have to visit, before it's too late. Lucy's not getting any younger.

HAY-ON-WYE TO KINGTON

Royal Oak Inn, Gladestry
Tel: 01544-370669
Pleasant pub just below Hergest Ridge, serving real ales and good food. A good refuelling stop before you have to cope with Mike Oldfield's music - or after you have done.

KINGTON

Olde Tavern, 22 Victoria Road
Tel: 01544-231384
If you can find it, it's allegedly Kington's link with the past, with two bars adorned with curios designed as a typical 19th century pub.

KNIGHTON

Horse and Jockey, Wylcym Place
Tel: 01547-520909
The interior décor suggests a youth-oriented clientele at certain times but not, I suspect, during the main part of the day. Handy because it's open all day.

George and Dragon, Broad Street
Tel: 01547-528532
Pleasant, old-fashioned sort of pub in the heart of the town. Serves good pub grub all week, including Sundays.

MONTGOMERY

Green Dragon, Montgomery
Tel: 1686-668359
Old 16th century coaching house, featuring beams allegedly nicked from Montgomery Castle. Excellent food and real ales. Swimming pool and sauna too, though you have to be a paying guest.

MONTGOMERY TO OSWESTRY

Powis Arms, Pool Quay
Tel: 01938-590253
Very special atmosphere - like being in your own home but with several beer pulls available. Liverpool in Wales.

Golden Lion Hotel, Four Crosses. Llanymynech
Tel: 01691-830295
Wonderfully-friendly pub, serving good food and real ales. Landlord and landlady are real characters.

Efel Inn, Trefonen
Tel: 01691-659840
Whatever you do, don't ask "Is efel in?" because they've heard it a thousand times. Just order an excellent sandwich and a cool pint.

OSWESTRY

Railway Inn, Beatrice Road
Tel: 1691-653489
Nothing special really, except that it serves good real ales.

OSWESTRY TO LLANGOLLEN

Aqueduct Inn, Holyhead Road, Froncysyllte
Tel: 01691-772481
Where I should have gone rather than the Trevor Inn. Excellent views of the aqueduct and good beers.

LLANGOLLEN

Sun Inn, 49 Regent Street
Tel: 01978-860233
Real-ale lovers' paradise, plus a range of unusual foreign beers. Excellent juke box, plus folk music on Wednesdays and live bands at other times.

LLANGOLLEN TO RUTHIN

The Crown Inn, Ruthin Road, Llandegla
Tel: 01978-790228
Very pleasant pub that breaks the journey between Llangollen and Ruthin and serves the wonderful John Willie's ales.

RUTHIN TO PRESTATYN

Downing Arms, Mold Road, Bodfari
Tel: 01745-710265
Pleasant country pub serving decent food and beer.

PRESTATYN

Offa's Tavern, 2-10 High Street
Tel: 01745 886046
Well, you have to go really, don't you? Though there's nothing specially to recommend it other than its name. And, to tell the truth, the best thing you can do in Prestatyn is get out of it.

PLACES TO STAY

CHEPSTOW

Upper Sedbury House
Sedbury Lane, Sedbury, Chepstow, NP16 7HN
Tel: 01291-627173
Email: map_home@hotmail.com
Web: www.smoothhound.co.uk/hotels/uppersed.html

CHEPSTOW TO MONMOUTH

Florence Country Hotel
Bigsweir, St Briavels, Gloucestershire, GL15 6QQ
Tel: 01594-530830
Email: enquiries@florencehotel.co.uk
Web: www.offas-dyke.co.uk/florencehotel

Old Brewery House
Brewery Yard, Redbrook on Wye, Monmouthshire, NP25 4LU
Tel: 01600-713819
Email: enquiries@oldbreweryhouse.com
Web: www.oldbreweryhouse.com

MONMOUTH

Burton Guesthouse
St James Square, Monmouth, Monmouthshire, NP25 3DN
Tel: 01600-714958
Email: rogerbanfield@aol.com

Verdi Bosco
65 Wonastow Road, Monmouth, Monmouthshire, NP25 5DG
Tel: 01600-714441
Web: www.offas-dyke.co.uk/verdibosco

MONMOUTH TO HAY-ON-WYE

Hunters Moon Pub
Llangattock, Lingoed, Monmouthshire, NP7 8RR
Tel: 01873-821499
Email: huntersmooninn@btinternet.com
Web: www.hunters-moon-inn.co.uk

Great Tre-Rhew Farm
Llanvetherine, Abergavenny, Monmouthshire, NP7 8RA
Tel: 01873-821268
Email: trerhew@btopenworld.com
Web: www.offas-dyke.co.uk/greattre-rhewfarm

The Old Pandy Inn
Hereford Road, Pandy, Abergavenny, NP7 8DR
Tel: 01873-890208
Email: enquiries@theoldpandyinn.co.uk
Web: www.theoldpandyinn.co.uk

Lancaster Arms Inn
Pandy, Abergavenny, Monmouthshire, NP7 8DW
Tel: 01873-890699
Email: lancaster-arms@supanet.com
Web: www.lancaster-arms.supanet.com

Half Moon Hotel
Llanthony, Abergavenny, Monmouthshire, NP7 7NN
Tel: 01873-890611
Email: halfmoonllanthony@talk21.com
Web: www.offas-dyke.co.uk/halfmoonhotel

HAY-ON-WYE

The Bear
Bear Street, Hay-on-Wye, Powys, HR3 5AN
Tel: 01497-821302
Email: jon@thebear-hay-on-wye.co.uk
Web: www.thebear-hay-on-wye.co.uk

The Baskerville Hall Hotel
Clyor Court, Hay on Way, HR3 5LE
Tel: 01497-820033
Email: paul@baskervillehall.co.uk
Web: www.offas-dyke.co.uk/baskervillehall.co.uk

La Fosse Guest House
Oxford Road, Hay-on-Wye, Herefordshire, HR3 5AJ
Tel: 01497-820613
Email: annabel@lafosse.co.uk
Web: www.Lafosse.co.uk

HAY-ON-WYE TO KINGTON

Offa's Dyke Lodge
Gladestry, nr Kington, Powys, HR5 3NR
Tel: 01544-370341
Email: steve@offtec.ltd.uk
Web: www.offas-dyke-lodge.co.uk

KINGTON

The Beacon
Bradnor Hill, Kington, Herefordshire, HR5 3RE
Tel: 01544-230182
Email: dickyhip@btinternet.com
Web: www.thetopbeacon.co.uk

Southbourne
Newton Lane, Kington, Herefordshire, HR5 3NF
Tel: 01544-231706
Email: geoff-patsy@btopenworld.com

The Burton Hotel
Mill Street, Kington, Herefordshire, HR5 3BQ
Tel: 01544-230323
Web: www.hotelherefordshire.co.uk

KNIGHTON

The Fleece House
Market Street, Knighton, Powys, LD7 1BB
Tel: 01547-520168
Email: fleecehouse@onetel.net.uk
Web: www.fleecehouse.co.uk

Offa's Dyke House
4 High Street, Knighton, Powys, LD7 1AT
Tel: 01547-529816
Email: odhgilly@tiscali.co.uk
Web: www.offas-dyke.co.uk/offasdykehouse

Westwood
Presteigne Road, Knighton, Powys, LD7 1HY
Tel: 01547-520317
Email: sharratt@westwoode.freeserve.co.uk
Web: www.offas-dyke.co.uk/westwood

KNIGHTON TO MONTGOMERY

Hendomen Farmhouse
Hendomen, Montgomery, Powys, SY15 6HB
Tel: 01686-668004
Email: bruce.lawson@btinternet.com
Web: www.offasdykepath.com

YHA Clun Mill
The Mill, Clun, Craven Arms, Shropshire, SY7 8NY
Tel: 0870 770 5916
Email: reservations@yha.org.uk

Newcastle Hall
Newcastle-on-Clun, Craven Arms, Shropshire, SY7 8QL
Tel: 01588-640350

Drewin Farm
Cwm, Churchstoke, Montgomery, SY15 6TW.
Tel: 01588-620325
Email: ceinwen@drewin.freeserve.co.uk

MONTGOMERY

Dragon Hotel
Montgomery, Powys, SY15 6PA
Tel: 01686-668359
Email: reception@dragonhotel.com
Web: www.dragonhotel.com

Little Brompton Farm
Montgomery, Powys, SY15 6HY
Tel: 01686-668371
Email: gaynor.brompton@virgin.net
Web: www.littlebromptonfarm.co.uk

MONTGOMERY TO OSWESTRY

1 Plas Cefn Holding
Heldre Lane, Buttington, Welshpool, SY21 8SX
Tel: 01938-570225

Lion Hotel
Llanymynech, Powys, SY22 6EJ
Tel: 01691-830234

The Royal Oak Hotel
Welshpool, Powys, SY21 7DG
Tel: 01938-552217
Email: oakwpool@aol.com

Severn Caravan Park
Forden, Welshpool, Powys, SY21 8RT
Tel: 01938-580238
Email: severncp@aol.com
Web: www.severnbunkhouse.co.uk

OSWESTRY

The Old Rectory
Glyn Road, Selattyn, Oswestry, SY10 7DH
Tel: 01691-659708

OSWESTRY TO LLANGOLLEN

Craignant Lodge
Craignant, Oswestry, Shropshire, SY10 7NS
Tel: 01691-718229

LLANGOLLEN

Abbey Grange Hotel
Llangollen, Denbighshire, LL20 8DD
Tel: 01978-860753
Email: sevans@netcomuk.co.uk

YHA Llangollen
Tyndwr Road, Llangollen, Denbighshire, LL20 8AR
Tel: 0870 770 5932
Email: llangollen@yha.org.uk

Oaklands
Llangollen Road, Trevor, Llangollen, LL20 7TG
Tel: 01978-820152
Email: oaklands_llangollen@fsmail.net

LLANGOLLEN TO RUTHIN

Saith Daran Farm
Llandegla, Wrexham, Denbighshire, LL11 3BA
Tel: 01978-790685
Email: welcome@saithdaran.freeserve.co.uk
Web: www.offas-dyke.co.uk/saithdaran

YHA Maeshafn
Maeshafn, Mold, Denbighshire, CH7 5LR
Tel: 0870 2412314/0870 770 594
Email: reservations@yha.org.uk

RUTHIN TO PRESTATYN

Fron Haul
Bodfari, Denbigh, Denbighshire, LL16 4DY
Tel: 01745-710301
Email: glad@fhsodham.fsnet.co.uk
Web: www.fron-haul.com

PRESTATYN

Traeth Ganol Hotel
41 Beach Rd West, Prestatyn, Denbighshire, LL19 7LL
Tel: 01745-853594
Email: info@hotel-prestatyn.co.uk

Roughsedge Guest House
26-28 Marine Road, Prestatyn, Denbighshire, LL19 7HD
Tel: 01745-887359
Email: roughsedge@ykubler.fsnet.co.uk

Also by Bob Bibby

GREY PAES AND BACON

Paying no heed to his gammy left knee, Wolverhampton-bred writer Bob Bibby sets out to discover the Black Country. He vows not to return until he's found out why the dialect is so mellifluous, where Black Country 'osses come from and what Lenny Henry was like as a schoolboy. Anxious about marching off into the unknown alone, he enlists ex-Scaffold member and Tiswas front man John Gorman as companion and bodyguard.

What ensues is a journey that is in turn entertaining, informative and wickedly irreverent. Join our unlikely heroes as they stamp on the stereotypes, sample the gastronomic delights, and unravel the mysteries, both past and present, of the Black Country.

Published by Eye Books Ltd.

ISBN 1 903070 06 6

"A wonderful read: witty, unsentimental and full of unforgettable thumbnail sketches."
Shropshire Review

"It's a bostin' book."
Carl Chinn - Radio WM

"If you're true Black Country, then read this. If not, read it anyway. It's a hoot."
Canal & Riverboat

DANCING WITH SABRINA

Following his last best-selling book *Grey Paes and Bacon*, when Bob took us around the canals of the Black Country, Bob dons his boots again to explore the river that runs past his doorstep in Bridgnorth, Shropshire.

Dancing with Sabrina takes us on a fantastic serpentine journey along a river from her source in the Welsh mountains to the Bristol Channel where she meets the sea. The Severn is England's longest river and takes her name from the Roman's given name of Sabrina, the secret love child of the ancient British King Locrine.

Bob whisks us back to discover the past and meet the villains, heroes and madmen that Sabrina has been witness to across the ages. He takes us through the towns and villages that have sprung up upon her banks and reveals their ancient secrets and folklore. He samples the modern day with his refreshingly simple needs and throws light on where to go and not to go, to eat, drink and visit.

For those who live in the embrace of Sabrina they will see the landscape of their home in an entirely new light and humour. For those who are new to the area *Dancing with Sabrina* will provide the impulse to visit and enjoy the richness of her heritage.

Published by Eye Books Ltd.

ISBN 1 903070 24 4

"One of the most interesting books to do with the river Severn that I have ever read...Bob Bibby's writing is reminiscent of Bill Bryson; he has a dry wit and a keen perception of detail that highlights the ordinary and elevates it."
Canal and Riverboat

"Bob Bibby is back on form with his latest travel book... The result is an enjoyable and entertaining read."
Shropshire Review

About Eye Books

Eye books is a young, dynamic publishing company that likes to break the rules. Our independence allows us to publish books which challenge the way people see things. It also means that we can offer new authors a platform from which they can shine their light and encourage others to do the same.

To date we have published 30 books that cover a number of genres including Travel, Biography, Adventure and History. Many of our books are experience driven. All of them are inspirational and life-affirming.

Frigid Women, for example, tells the story of the world-record making first all female expedition to the North Pole. A fifty year-old mother of three who had recently recovered from a mastectomy, and her daughter are the authors neither had ever written a book before. Sue Riches is now both author and highly sought after motivational speaker.

We also publish thematic anthologies, such as The Tales from Heaven and Hell series, for those who prefer the short story format. Here everyone has the chance to get their stories published and win prizes such as flights to any destination in the world.

And here's what makes us really different: As well as publishing books, Eye Books has set up a club for like-minded people and is in the process of developing a number of initiatives and services for its community of members. After all, the more you put into life, the more you get out of it.

Please visit www.eye-books.com for further information.

Eye Club Membership

Each month, we receive hundreds of enquiries' from people who have read our books, discovered our website or entered our competitions. All of these people have certain things in common; a desire to achieve, to extend the boundaries of everyday life and to learn from others' experiences.

Eye Books has, therefore, set up a club to unite these like-minded people. It is a community where members can exchange ideas, contact authors, discuss travel, both future and past as well as receive information and offers from ourselves.

Membership is free.

Benefits of the Eye Club

As a member of the Eye Club:

• You are offered the invaluable opportunity to contact our authors directly.
• You will be able to receive a regular newsletter, information on new book releases and company developments as well as discounts on new and past titles.
• You can attend special member events such as book launches, author talks and signings.
• Receive discounts on a variety of travel related products and services from Eye Books partners.
• In addition, you can enjoy entry into Eye Books competitions including the ever popular Heaven and Hell series and our monthly book competition.

To register your membership, simply visit our website and register on our club pages: www.eye-books.com.

New Titles

Riding the Outlaw Trail - Simon Casson
A true story of an epic horseback journey by two Englishmen from
Mexico to Canada, across 2,000 miles of some of America's most
difficult terrain. Their objective? To retrace the footsteps of those
legendary real life bandits Butch Cassidy and the Sundance Kid, by
riding the outlaw trails they rode more than a century ago.
ISBN: 1 903070 228. Price £9.99.

Desert Governess - Phyllis Ellis
Phyllis, a former Benny Hill actress, takes on a new challenge when
she becomes a governess to the Saudi Arabian Royal family. In this
frank personal memoir, she gives us an insider's view into the Royal
family and a woman's role in this mysterious kingdom.
ISBN: 1 903070 015. Price £9.99.

Last of the Nomads - W. J. Peasley
Warri and Yatungka were the last of the desert nomads to live
permanently in the traditional way. Their deaths marked the end
of a tribal lifestyle that stretched back more than 30,000 years. The
Last of the Nomads tells of an extraordinary journey in search of
Warri and Yatungka, their rescue and how they survived alone for
thirty years in the unrelenting Western Desert region of Australia.
ISBN: 1 903070 325. Price £9.99.

All Will Be Well - Michael Meegan
So many self help books look internally to provide inspiration,
however this book looks at how love and compassion when given
out to others, can act as a better antidote to the human condition
than trying to inwardly solve feelings of discontentment.
ISBN: 1 903070 279. Price £9.99.

First Contact - Mark Anstice

This is a true story of a modern day exploration by two young adventurers and the discovery of cannibal tribes in the 21st century. An expedition far more extraordinary than they had ever imagined, one that would stretch them, their friendship and their equipment to the limits.

ISBN: 1 903070 260. Price £9.99.

Further Travellers' Tales From Heaven and Hell Part 3 - Various

This is the third book in the series, after the first two best selling Travellers' Tales from Heaven and Hell. It is an eclectic collection of over a hundred anecdotal travel stories which will enchant you, shock you and leave you in fits of laughter!

ISBN: 1 903070 112. Price £9.99.

The Good Life - Dorian Amos

Needing a change and some adventure, Dorian and his wife searched their world atlas and decided to sell up and move to Canada. Having bought Pricey the car, Boris Lock their faithful dog, a canoe and their fishing equipment they set off into the Yukon Wilderness to find a place they could call home.

ISBN: 1 903070 309. Price £9.99.

Baghdad Business School - Heyrick Bond Gunning

A camp bed, ten cans of baked beans, some water and $25,000 is all that was needed to set up an International Business in Iraq. The book chronicles an amusing description of the trials and tribulations of doing business in an environment where explosions and shootings are part of everyday life, giving the reader a unique insight into what is really happening in this country.

ISBN: 1 903070 333. Price £9.99.

Green Oranges on Lion Mountain - Emily Joy
Armed with a beginner's guide to surgery, GP Emily Joy took up
her VSO posting at a remote hospital in Sierra Leone. As she set off
into the unknown, action, adventure and romance were high on
her agenda; rebel forces and the threat of civil war were not.
ISBN: 1 903070 295. Price £9.99.

The Con Artist Handbook - Joel Levy
Get wise with The Con Artist's Handbook as it blows the lid on the
secrets of the successful con artist and his con games. Get inside
the hustler's head and find out what makes him tick; Learn how the
world's most infamous scams are set up and performed; Peruse the
career profiles of the most notorious scammers and hustlers of all time;
Learn to avoid the modern-day cons of the e-mail and Internet age.
ISBN: 1 903070 341. Price £9.99.

The Forensics Handbook - Pete Moore
The Forensic Handbook is the most up-to-date log of forensic
techniques available. Discover how the crime scene is examined
using examples of some of the most baffling crimes; Learn
techniques of lifting, comparing and identifying prints; Calculate
how to examine blood splatter patterns; Know what to look for
when examining explosive deposits, especially when terrorist
activity is suspected.
Learn how the Internet is used to trace stalkers.
ISBN: 1 903070 35X. Price £9.99.

Book Microsites

If you are interested in finding out more about this book please visit our book microsite:

www.eye-books.com/specialoffa/home.htm

We have also created microsites for a number of our other new books including:

Riding The Outlaw Trail
Desert Governess
The Last of the Nomads
First Contact
The Good Life
No Socks No Sex
Baghdad Business School

For details on these sites and others which we are developing please visit our main website:

www.eye-books.com

Special Offers and Promotions

We are offering our club members and people who have read this book the opportunity to take advantage of promotions on our other books by buying direct from us.

For information on these special offers please visit the following page of our website:

www.eye-books.com/promotions.htm